NO LOCKED DOORS!

NO LOCKED DOORS!

MASTER THE KEYS TO
TRANSFORM **PROBLEMS**
INTO **POSSIBILITIES**

GREGORY SMITH

Copyright © 2023 Gregory Smith
All rights reserved.

NO LOCKED DOORS!
Master the Keys to Transform Problems into Possibilities

FIRST EDITION

ISBN 978-1-5445-4264-5 Hardcover
      978-1-5445-4262-1 Paperback
      978-1-5445-4263-8 Ebook

*This one's for you, my readers, and for those
I met along my journey, who discovered they had the
keys within themselves to unlock most any door.*

*And for my family—my wife, Katherine,
who has unwaveringly supported me for half a century,
and our two daughters, who have heard
it all too many times!*

This book contains stories and interactions
that reflect the author's personal and honest recollections
and experiences over time.
While all of these events occurred, names,
characters, businesses, and locations have been changed
to protect the identities of individuals and
businesses throughout the book.

CONTENTS

FOREWORD ix
By Kasim Aslam, Mentee, Mentor, Serial Entrepreneur, and Friend

INTRODUCTION 1

Chapter 1
BRASS TACKS 9

Chapter 2
FAILING FRENCH 23

Chapter 3
WHAT IF I DON'T WANT TO BE AN ADMIRAL? 35

Chapter 4
HAVE YOU LOST YOUR MIND? 47

Chapter 5
WAIT FOR IT 63

Chapter 6
CAN YOU SPELL PRESIDENT? 77

Chapter 7
CHANGING PERCEPTIONS 91

Chapter 8
STICK TO YOUR KNITTING 105

Chapter 9
SKY'S THE LIMIT 115

Chapter 10
WHEN TO QUIT 123

Chapter 11
WHAT ARE YOU DOING HERE? 135

Chapter 12
ICEBERG, RIGHT AHEAD! 147

Chapter 13
A WORKOUT BUDDY 159

Chapter 14
NEVER TOO LATE 171

Chapter 15
GETTING OLDER IN A LIVING WAY 183

CONCLUSION 195

ACKNOWLEDGMENTS 201

ABOUT THE AUTHOR 205

FOREWORD

By Kasim Aslam, Mentee, Mentor, Serial Entrepreneur, and Friend

Greg Smith is a lot of things: Father and Grandfather, Husband, Entrepreneur, Mentor, Author. But the first and most important thing he's been for me is a thief.

I met Greg almost by accident. At the time, I had a huge chip on my shoulder: I had grown up "poor," raised by a blind, single mother living on social security disability. My little brother and I were effectively welfare babies, and I just loved to tell anyone who would listen about how hard we'd had it. It was my identity.

When I first met Greg, I had no business being in the same room as a man like him. He was (and still is) one of the most accomplished people I had ever met. He was a paragon of excellence, and I was a nineteen-year-old dropout, a compulsive liar, and (pathetically) a wanna-be thug. And yet, Greg decided to take me under his wing. I used to think he took pity on me. As I've gotten to know him, I believe he was just doing what he always does: care, love, empower.

The first thing Greg stole from me was my fantasy about being a victim. But, in typical Greg fashion, he didn't sit me down for a lecture on gratitude; instead, Greg and his wife, Katie, took me on a trip to Egypt. I had never traveled internationally, had barely traveled outside of the American Southwest. It was an absolute culture shock.

I saw children no older than five living on the streets, starving and alone. This was true poverty. I had nothing on these kids, and Greg knew it. He knew that with greater perspective, I could begin to see my own life differently, to live with appreciation, perspective, and confidence—not as a victim of my circumstances. But he didn't tell me. He showed me. That's how he works.

When I started my business, like all entrepreneurs, my goal was to be a self-made success. It's not enough to climb the mountain; we need everyone to know we did it on our own: "Mommy and Daddy never gave me a damn thing. I built this thing from the ground up. Blah, blah, blah."

The problem with that dream: I had Greg. Greg was there when I needed it most—when I had no clue what I needed—and helped me find my way. He mentored me, coached me, and taught me: gently, kindly, and humbly. He didn't solve my problems for me. He was, and still is, a trusted guide.

He didn't steal my right to call myself self-made. He stole my illusion that such a thing as self-made even exists. We all need help. Mentorship. Guidance. Tough love. We can't make it without these things. And, miraculously, they're readily available, if we know where to look.

If there's one thing I'll say for myself, I've always sought out the wisdom of others. Some of the smartest, most accomplished people in history are sitting there, on a shelf, waiting to give us literal step-by-step guidance. It horrifies me to think about how few people take them up on the offer.

Maybe you weren't as lucky as I was. Maybe you didn't have a Greg Smith waltz into your life and spend almost twenty years helping you accomplish your biggest goals. That doesn't mean you can't benefit from his wisdom, because he took the time to write this book.

And let me tell you, this man has wisdom.

People talk all the time about "overcoming problems." But a lot of the time, this feels impossible. You get a flat tire on the side of the road and you're going to miss your flight. That's a problem, and most of us would just get stuck there. Not Greg. He will find a way to not only fix it but to make true connections (or a ton of money) along the way.

Making a problem disappear is magic, but turning a problem into an opportunity—that's alchemy. And Greg Smith is an alchemist.

But I also know Greg's level of greatness is something that can be studied and learned, something that others can understand and embody. It's accessible. And if we were each to adopt just a fraction of Greg's intentionality, creativity, and humility—the world would be better for it.

But you have to really want it. Limitations are things we impose on ourselves to protect our ego. They're comfortable friends that whisper reassurances about how impossible things are and how few choices we really have.

My hope is that in these pages, you truly encounter my friend Greg, and you allow him the opportunity to steal from you too. Steal your reliance on limiting beliefs. Steal your excuses about what's possible.

I hope that you get to sit at his feet and learn from a true sage. That you get to witness his uncanny ability to solve the most ridiculous problems. That you get to marvel at his ability to connect with people, to make them feel like the only person in the whole world. That you laugh. My hope is that you see things differently—whatever that means for you—and that you will gain just a little bit more hope, perspective, and inspiration.

Because for all Greg has taken from me, he's given me so much more. And chief among those gifts is the sincere belief that I can succeed.

And you can too.

INTRODUCTION

I was managing a bank holding company, with community banks across multiple states, for a high-net-worth family when I found myself—literally overnight—running a commercial airline.

My boss at the time had purchased a small nonunion charter commercial airline. The purchase saddled the company with millions in acquisition debt and positioned the airline in an ugly battle with large predatory commercial airlines. Needless to say, the airline was in desperate need of an overhaul. One night—within a year of the purchase—the president (also a pilot and co-founder of the company) had just landed a plane. Three hours later, he found himself on an operating room table with a 94 percent blockage in his heart. He didn't make it.

"What should we do?" I asked my boss. "I can hire some of the best airline guys in the country. I'll find them."

"We don't need any more aviation people, Greg," My boss said. "We need someone with a different experience, a different point of view. You've worked for me now for ten years. You get over there and figure it out."

So, I showed up the next day and stood in front of the COO and co-founder, with no experience, no knowledge, no clue how to run an airline. "I'm Greg Smith," I said. "Our boss sent me to help you through this transition." *Oh, by the way, I'm the new co-president with you. And oh, by the way, I'm the new vice chairman of your board. But let's look at this as a partnership, buddy.*

He barely looked at me. "We really don't need you here," he said. "We can figure it out ourselves."

But the reality was that the guy running the show was gone and the COO got a field promotion. He had just lost his friend and business partner, and said business needed to grow substantially and profitably to service its new acquisition debt. None of us knew that after solving these immediate problems and expanding the fleet, the economy would hit a major downturn and the company would have to make a major reduction in workforce. At that point, the co-founder needed more than a *little* help.

He said, "Let me show you your office, Mr. Smith. It's right next to mine."

I opened the door to see a rusted six-foot-tall metal shelf full of cleaning chemicals and a drain in the center of the floor next to a leaking, dirty mop bucket.

"OK," I said, "I get it."

I turned around and went right out to the ramp where the planes were, put on some dirty coveralls, and started tossing bags with the ground operations agents. I was angry. Absolutely livid. And I didn't know what to do. But I knew I had to fix this. I had to figure out a way to get this partner co-founder to do what I knew he needed to do—not because I told him to but because he *chose* to do it.

A WAY THROUGH

When I arrived on scene, I found a locked door—in the form of a fully grown man who did not want my help, advice, or presence.

Perhaps you could even say there were *several* doors: all locked, deadbolted, and chained (except for the mop closet, of course). This was not going to be easy, and I didn't have a magic key that could open every one of these locks, not even one. I didn't have a quick fix. I didn't even have a sledgehammer. I had to find a way through, carefully and considerately. I had to pick the lock with a fine wire to align the mechanism and open the door without forcing it.

Spoiler alert (and more on this story to come): we not only saved the company, but we grew it. We recovered from a horrendous economic downturn, added to the fleet, and hired back all the employees that we had to let go. We didn't just fix it. We made it better. And we took care of every single person in the process, rewarding the employees with a significant profits interest that provided over $30 million in retirement benefits and kept the unions voted out. (I'm pleased to say those funds would become a lifesaver for these treasured friends and employees when a far worse fate befell the airline under different owners years down the road.)

Do you know how long this took? Years—nine of them—to realize and reap the full benefits of this overhaul. It required a great deal of innovation and patience. A whole lot of humility and collaboration. Lots of question-asking and resilience and vision-casting: just a few of the invaluable keys I've collected over the years that I'm about to share with you in the next two hundred pages or so.

MY KEY RING

When Kasim Aslam, a friend who you'll hear more about in later chapters, first told me I should write a book, he gifted me a leather journal and a way-too-fancy pen. At the time, I didn't take him seriously. I never even cracked the journal open. From time to time, Kasim would ask me how my book was coming along, and I would let him know, "Um, I haven't really started it yet."

Turns out, Kasim was very serious about this book-writing thing. A few years later—realizing that I wasn't going to make any headway on this project on my own—I received a big blue box from Scribe Media, with a note that said:

> If ever there was a story that needed to be told, it is yours.
>
> To that end: I've engaged with the world authorities in publishing to help bring your book to life.

Now I had no excuse. Now I actually had a team of people who were not only going to hold me accountable but who were going to draw the dang thing out of me. I would write a book, whether I wanted to or not! Thank you, Kasim, from the very bottom of my heart.

I don't consider myself an expert in anything per se, but I have become known as "a fixer." I love a good, seemingly impossible problem, and probably because of this, I have found myself in some pretty wacky situations throughout the years. I've made difficult decisions, learned from my failures, realized the value of relationships, and—thankfully—experienced a great deal of success along the way. There were plenty of moments that I could have (and wanted to) jump off the boat. But the biggest lesson I learned, and therefore the biggest message I have to share with you is: treat challenges as opportunities.

Problems are simply possibilities in disguise.

With this perspective, I have gotten to be a part of so many unbelievably positive outcomes. In fact, I have a drawer in my desk full of cards and mementos just saying "thank you" to me—little old Greg Smith from Bloomington, Minnesota. That's humbling and it's been an honor, a true honor, to help so many people find answers that they mostly had inside themselves.

NO SHORTCUTS

We all face locked doors. In reality, our lives are really a series of challenges. Once we unlock one door, voila! There's another! How you choose to work through them sets you apart, defines you, determines your future.

So often, we get in the way of ourselves. Whether it's lack of confidence, fear of failing, an overinflated ego, loneliness, hopelessness, or just plain laziness—we give up too soon. We stand on the sidelines and wait for someone else to unlock the door. We ignore the door, forget about what's on the other side. Or perhaps we look for a shortcut, a way around, a different direction to head that isn't so hard or complicated, that doesn't require so much from us. Realistically, the odds of finding an alternative route or a shortcut through our locked doors are not good and full of unnecessary risks.

The only viable way is *through*. And while your process could be one of frustration, resentment, and resignation, I want to invite you on a different journey—one of creativity, self-discovery, and new heights of success. There's more for you. There is a better way.

BECOMING A LOCKSMITH

I want to help you reframe how you view problems in your life. I truly believe that we are meant not only to solve problems but to view them as opportunities, to transform them into possibilities, opening the door wide to a life of happiness, fulfillment, gratitude, connection, and belief.

This book is a series of short stories, a collection of some of the doors I have had the privilege of unlocking. I'll share my experiences with merciless teachers, government regulators, business moguls, big-time deal makers, bankers, and some bad guys too. I'll show you how it worked for me, and I hope you are able to integrate this knowledge into your own life.

I want to be forthcoming here. I am a white, heterosexual, able-bodied man who grew up in a middle-class family, from a small town in middle America. There are obvious privileges and advantages that my skin color, gender, abilities, sexual orientation, upbringing, and background have provided. I don't deny this. And I think it would be a disservice to all of my readers not to acknowledge this. I am aware of the challenges that underrepresented people face, challenges that I will never know firsthand. But I believe that the lessons I've learned, the challenges I've overcome, and the values I've put to the test are applicable to any human. Many of the tools I'll share are the very keys that have helped me understand and connect with people that look, think, act, and feel differently than I do. Regardless of our differences, I hope that you can find something of value in these pages, something that can guide your next steps.

I am more of a "shower" than a "teller" in normal life. But it turns out that this is a book, so inevitably there will be a bit of telling, as well. These—what I like to call—"gg moments" (short for Grandpa Greg) will begin with a question because I think we can access most of the answers we are looking for within ourselves. No one else can tell you what is most important, who you want to be, what keeps you up at night, and the right decision to make. You ultimately have to ask and answer for yourself. I am simply here as a guide.

I believe we are all key masters or locksmiths, if you will. I believe each and every one of us has the tools to access or create the keys that we need to unlock the doors in front of us. These keys take different shapes and sizes, but they can often be used on several different doors. Finding them, uncovering them, requires patience and perseverance. Sometimes we have to look at the lock from all angles, envision the door opening before us, and imagine the world that might be on the other side.

My hope is that you will find yourself in these pages. My goal is not to toot my own horn and tell you how amazing I am. I actually think I'm quite a normal guy, with a unique perspective and a few years of experience under my belt. I hope you'll start to see that you, too, have what it takes—the confidence, the skills, the patience, the forethought, the power—to become the person you hope to be and to make decisions based on that vision. And perhaps even help others along the way.

You'll see: the answers are inside of you. Now let's unlock some doors.

Chapter 1

BRASS TACKS

WHEN I WAS SEVEN YEARS OLD, in 1957, my dad came home one day with a brand-new TV set. I remember thinking it was enormous, too big for our small home on Bloomington Avenue in Bloomington, Minnesota. He set the TV box on the floor, went out to the shed, and returned with a saw, toolbox, and pencil in hand. He measured the TV screen, drew a rectangle onto our living room wall, and proceeded to build the TV into the wall so that only the screen was visible. Later that evening, my family squeezed onto our plaid couch, five in a row, and watched *Leave it to Beaver* on the world's first-ever flat-screen TV. Meanwhile, the back of our built-in television shared space with the furnace in the utility room.

This same year, my parents decided that I should take piano lessons, likely motivated by the reality that I wasn't quite excelling at sports as they had hoped and therefore needed some other outlet to expend time and energy. And, of course, if I was going to take piano lessons, I had to have some way to practice. So, my dad purchased a piano—or perhaps I should say, my dad bought something that *resembled* a piano because it was really eighty-eight different pieces, and none of them quite connected. While it was made of wood, it had unfortunately been spray-painted an awful grayish texture, and the entire family was appalled by its appearance.

This same modest house certainly did not contain enough space to store an upright 1890s piano. So again, out came the toolbox, and my dad and I proceeded to carve another hole—this time into the basement wall—where we pushed the piano. The only thing sticking out was the keyboard.

My parents enrolled me in lessons with Mrs. Bonfi, an elderly woman whose home was almost too far to ride my bike, but not far enough. With my lesson book in the basket, I pedaled my way there. Perhaps I would have taken to playing the piano immediately had it not been for Mrs. Bonfi. Unfortunately, I began associating piano-playing with the nauseating odor of old-lady body lotion and the feeling of sticky keys covered in a film of facial cosmetics. Her surly black cat would walk across the top of the piano while I stumbled through a seven-year-old's version of Beethoven, music I hated playing as much as I hated stepping over the threshold of Mrs. Bonfi's home. Maybe I could have overlooked her nauseating odor, but she was grumpy and mean too.

INNOVATION

When I'd try to practice this same music at home (in a valiant attempt to avoid a ruler slap on the back of my hand at the following week's lesson), all I could think about was having to return to that dreaded house and perform in her disastrous recitals. So, in the same spirit of ingenuity that my dad had enlisted to invent the world's first flat-screen, I took a box of brass tacks and hammered one into each of the eighty-eight keys.

After that, instead of the soft, melodic tone that pianos are known for, my piano was loud and emitted a one-of-a-kind honky-tonk sound—much to my parents' dismay—and one that was so far from the sound I associated with Mrs. Bonfi that I found a new sense of joy and freedom in learning this brilliant instrument! God forbid, I had money to purchase honky-tonk sheet music, and I certainly wasn't going to attempt Mozart in honky-tonk form, so I resorted to listening to the radio and mimicking what I heard. I called it Modified Mozart! My parents were stunned speechless, realizing the piano's mellifluous tone would never be the same again. I might as well have had a drumset.

Mind you, I was seven years old. I haven't a clue what was actually going through my head. But I know that I wasn't questioning whether or not I deserved to be happy. I knew that I didn't like playing the piano at Mrs. Bonfi's. I also knew I was stuck playing the piano because my parents ruled the roost. So, I took it into my own hands to find happiness in this endeavor. I honestly think that we could all stand to adopt a little more of this seven-year-old-Greg's mentality. There is plenty of sadness in this world, plenty of suffering, but I believe we have the right to have a happy and fulfilling life. Many times, it's a matter of finding it, creating it, and—maybe most of all—feeling like we *deserve* it.

When I changed the texture of the music, it became more interesting to me. Suddenly, I liked playing the piano—no, I *loved* it—and I also realized I could play by ear. Discerning this required seven-year-old Greg to get creative, to take a risk, and to think for myself. And here's what I learned: innovation beats boredom and repetition every time.

This is a lesson I've carried with me throughout my entire life. Not everything has to be scripted. If we follow everything by the book, the chances of us failing are pretty high because the standards of the book are really someone else's expectations. And living by someone else's rules is boring. We all have to answer to someone—whether it's an employer, a parent, a spouse, a shareholder, or a mean piano teacher—but we can still find a way to maintain and express our own creative ingenuity.

We can often beat monotony with a few little creative tweaks and twists and turns: by adding our own flavor, by trying an unwritten recipe, by hammering some brass tacks into our piano keys and changing the tune.

HIDDEN TALENT

Unfortunately, my musical innovation did not put a stop to lessons at Mrs. Bonfi's. But the sound of my makeshift instrument drove my parents so crazy that my dad decided to replace it with an electronic organ that would be stored in the main part of the house, instead of relegated to the dark, lonely basement. Along with the purchase of this brand-new organ, the vendor offered three free lessons, so off I went to Swanee Swanson's Northwest Lowrey Organ Studio to learn how to operate the complicated assortment of buttons, pedals, and not one but *two* keyboards.

Swanee Swanson's organ studio smelled like heaven. The organ itself smelled like heaven, with its electronic bulbs and whirling speakers. And the experience couldn't have been any more different from playing an ancient 1894 upright Fisher piano. With this one instrument, I could articulate all sorts of sounds! I could take a song and play it ten times, and it would never sound the same, which was great for me because one thing I had discovered was my love for improvisation. I wasn't all that great at reading sheet music, and the organ offered me the freedom to set that sheet music aside and have some fun.

During my second lesson, Swanee Swanson himself popped by, an older, chubby man with big, black glasses and a booming voice. He said, "Hey kid! How many lessons have you had?"

I said, "This is my second lesson, sir."

"Are you going to stick around and take some more lessons?" he asked.

"Um, probably not," I replied.

He asked me when my next lesson was and at my third and final lesson, there was Mr. Swanson, big grin on his face, applauding my eight-and-a-half-year-old efforts.

"What are you doing next Sunday?" he asked me and my dad.

I said, "Playing baseball."

My dad said, "Why do you ask?"

"Well, I think Greg should come over here on Sunday. I'd like him to play for some people."

My dad said, "He'll be here."

Of course, I didn't want to do it. I was trying to get out of the whole ordeal, put Mrs. Bonfi and her smelly odors behind me. But I didn't seem to have a real choice in the matter. So when the following Sunday rolled around, much to my dismay, my dad and I drove to Swanee Swanson's. But when we walked through the familiar doors, we couldn't believe our eyes—the entire store had been transformed into a television studio! There was a big tent and bright lights and a fancy backdrop. And in the middle of all this hoopla was an organ on a small stage, decked out with a microphone, cameras, and all.

This was live television!

After Mr. Swanson introduced us to the crew, the cameraman asked me, "What are you going to play?"

I said, "Well, I've only had three free lessons so far."

"Save that for when the camera starts rolling. I'll ask you about that. But what are you going to play?"

I said, "Uhhhh... 'Five Foot Two'... 'Twelfth Street Rag'... and 'Blue Champagne.' Those are the three songs I've learned."

"That sounds good," he replied.

When the cameras were on, Mr. Swanson introduced himself and said, "I'm coming live to you this Sunday morning at ten o'clock with our very special guest, little Greg Smith from Bloomington, Minnesota. Greg, how old are you?"

"I'm eight and a half. I'm almost nine," I said.

"And how many lessons have you had on the Lowrey organ?"

"Three, sir."

Mr. Swanson said, "What are you going to play for us today, Greg?"

So I told him my list of songs and he said, "Take it away."

I pounded out the three songs I knew. Everyone in the studio was anticipating a typical eight-year-old-beginner rendition of Chopsticks, thinking that I would barely be able to strike a chord. Boy, were they surprised! I brought the house down! Now, of course I never got to tell anyone I had a year and a half of classical training from Mrs. Bonfi. That detail never came out (Mr. Swanson made sure of it). In everyone's minds, I was a pure prodigy. And for the next year, I would head to Swanee Swanson's Northwest Lowrey Organ

Studio to play on live television a couple of Sundays a month. And best of all, I got to put Mrs. Bonfi's lessons out of my mind.

HELLO, EGO

Now, when I walked into the organ-studio-turned-live-television-studio, I can only imagine how overwhelmed I truly was. I had certainly not signed up for a Sunday-morning TV special for the whole town to see. I had no clue what I was getting myself into, nor did I know if I even had what it took to get up there and perform in front of a live audience, and God knows who else was watching. It could have been a disaster (and that would have been a great story too).

This was likely the first time (unbeknownst to me) I experienced that stress is invigorating to me. I was able to listen to and feel what was inside of me and turn it into something powerful and inspiring. I had my dad there, and I knew I didn't want to disappoint him. And I knew I didn't want to quit on myself. I wanted to see what I could do. So I took a risk, stepped on stage, pounded on that organ, and relished in the victory.

We all have an ego, and it can be our friend or our enemy, whether we're seven years old or seventy-two! Many of us have our egos out in front of us all of the time, offering the world a shallow characterization of who we think we are or who we want others to believe us to be. On that Sunday morning, I was just beginning to get to know my ego—I liked the attention. I liked being the person in the middle of the room. My ego was saying, *Let's have some fun with this. Let's show them what you can do.*

At this point in my young life, my ego had to pull me along a little bit. It had to convince me to get on the stage, to take a risk, to try something new. Later in life, I would have to learn to manage this same ego, to let it go when it wasn't serving me. One of the necessities in a happy, successful life is realizing that we have a choice: to hold our egos out front or to check them at the door and present our true selves to the world, openly and honestly (more on this to come). But there are times in our lives when our egos help us move in the right direction, help us uncover what we're made of, and explore our potential.

I had no idea I was capable of capturing an audience's attention. Prior to this experience, I was just little Greg Smith who couldn't hit a T-ball far enough to make it to first base. Little Greg Smith who hated the smell of Mrs. Bonfi's house but sure could hammer out some honky-tonk in my own home. Had my ego never convinced me to step foot on that tiny stage, I would have never known that this (amateur) musician existed inside of me.

PERCOLATION

There's a great story I heard about Frank Lloyd Wright, who took a commission to build a house in the 1930s called Fallingwater, outside of Pittsburgh, Pennsylvania. Wright went and stood over the waterfall with Edgar J. Kaufmann, original owner of the home, and envisioned how the house would look. After that day, four years went by. Wright was all over the place, taking various jobs and commissions, and he made no tangible plans for Faillingwater—no drawings, no crew, no nothing.

Then one day, Kaufmann called him up out of the blue and told him he needed the plans, that it was time. Wright told him that they were nearly done, no problem, and apologized for the delay.

Kaufmann said he was on his way from Milwaukee, Wisconsin, and that he would be at Wright's studio in Spring Green, Wisconsin, within a few hours. So Wright got to work, for real. He gathered his apprentices, his mechanics, and his engineers. He started drawing lines with chalk, tearing off sheets, and passing them to the right hands. His people started figuring out how to make it work, tweaking, redesigning, bringing it to life. Wright finished hanging those drawings all over his studio right when Kaufmann was pulling up the drive.

Kaufmann took a look at the haphazard drawings on the walls and fell in love with the house, on sight.

Wright said, "We're going to need to make a few edits here and there."

Kaufmann said, "Nope, we're not making any changes. We're going to build it just the way you drew it. I love it."

Now, they've had to rebuild this house more than twenty times, but that's not the point. The point is, Wright had these plans up his sleeve all along. He stood over the waterfall that day, saw the home in his head, and carried this knowledge and vision with him for four years before putting pen to paper. It was all inside of him; he just wasn't ready to produce it (until he was ready, or should I say forced?).

The same was true for me with this book. When Kasim first threw out the idea of me writing a book, I didn't believe I had it in me. But here I am, writing it. This book was inspired by a lifetime of percolation—lessons I learned, experiences I had, people I met, failures, victories, tears, and joys. It wasn't until I sat down to write that I truly realized all that I could put into words. These words were tucked away inside of the experiences themselves.

I think this is true for every single one of us. You have something inside of you, and if you can find the patience to let it simmer and the courage to bring it forth, you may have the opportunity to do something spectacular with your life. This process requires a great deal of self-discipline and perseverance—with *ourselves*—which is something that most of us struggle with. We want instant gratification. We don't want to wait for the magic to happen. We want to succeed, to be recognized, to shine.

Sometimes when we think we're nearly out of time, it's pretty easy to quit before we get around to doing what we said we would do. We let a task go as if it wasn't really all that important to complete. We might justify this choice to ourselves and others: "Sorry, I just ran out of time." If it was a personal matter—a daily workout, a phone call, an item on a to-do list—then only we know we missed it. No big deal.

But consider that time can also be a catalyst to inspire your best work. Perhaps you put off a project because you weren't really feeling it, but suddenly it's crunch time. You have limited hours or minutes to get it done. If you press into these moments and choose to stay in it (instead of quitting or giving up), odds are you may not only get it done, but it may be your very best work yet. Improvisation is a spontaneous expression of something you had inside you, maybe for a long time. And, when the pressure is on, sometimes the brilliance just oozes out. It could be a joke or a story. It could be a term paper. It could be a plan on how to save a business in dire straits. Or it might be a pathway to saving a friendship or marriage.

I had a year and a half of miserable lessons with Mrs. Bonfi before discovering the joy of playing an instrument, nearly complete improvisation, and performing in front of adults. Oftentimes, as the stakes get higher and the goals get loftier, this process of percolation takes longer. Don't give up too soon.

I still play the piano today. So much so that when I built a home in Scottsdale, Arizona, in 2005, I acquired a very rare Steinway grand piano and have many fond memories of playing for guests, concert-hall style, in that home. It now lives in my daughter's house in Minneapolis, where my eight-year-old grandson is learning to play —oh how life comes full circle! (You better believe I am cheering on his efforts, just like my dad and Mr. Swanson and all of those Sunday-morning viewers did for me.) It goes to show that we absolutely never know what skills, relationships, and experiences will shape the rest of our lives. While you certainly won't find me playing the organ on your Sunday-morning TV, it's a hobby that taught me many things as a child and one that continues to bring joy and color into my life today.

A KEY: INNOVATION

Question: Are you open to changing your perspective?

In the middle of these piano lessons with Mrs. Bonfi, I was a bit stuck. I wanted to please my parents by continuing with the lessons, so I didn't want to quit. But I also hated the lessons themselves. I was forced to find a creative solution to my own predicament. And while our adult problems cannot likely be fixed with a box of brass tacks (but by all means, you're welcome to give it a try), this idea of innovation can go a long way.

Whether you're a CEO or a new parent or an eight-year-old kid, we all need creativity, inspiration, and ideas that make our world and our lives better. Innovation begins with curiosity: What is the problem that needs solving? How can I play a part in making it better or eliminating it altogether? And maybe, am I willing to change my perspective?

Often the solution we are looking for is not the most obvious one. The most obvious solution to my predicament at the age of eight was to quit and to deal with the consequences of letting my parents down. They still would have loved me and encouraged me to find some other hobby. But do you see the problem? I would have missed out on so much! I stayed in the game— I let some percolation happen—and in the end, I built a ton of self-confidence and discovered an incredible amount of joy in playing the keyboard.

The same is true for you. Taking the easy way out, avoiding the locked door, asking someone else for the key—these are all obvious solutions *around* the problem that do not open doors to more opportunities, talent, and growth.

Innovation requires risk. It's a commitment to trial and error. You won't always find the solution the first time around, but you have to remember that you do have what it takes to find your way through. Once you've identified the actual problem, sit with it. Think about the most obvious solutions. And then let it sit for a while longer. See what bubbles up from inside of you. You likely have more ability in you to find an innovative solution than you give yourself credit for.

But, at the end of the day, you have to want it. Not just hope that you can do it, but faith that you *will* do it. You have to want to solve problems, to win, to open the doors that are in front of you. And I will say, uncovering creative solutions is rewarding and enriching. It will build your self-confidence, it will attract success, and it will set you apart as a creative, capable person.

Chapter 2

FAILING FRENCH

I ROLLED INTO LITTLE AUGSBURG COLLEGE, which sits in the shadows of the University of Minnesota, with a great big ego and no questions about whether I would succeed. You see, I had some pretty nice accomplishments under my belt by then: I had graduated high school with honors, led the high school marching band as its president and on the field as its drum major, and even had a high school sweetheart to speak of. I had a decent job, a small scholarship, and was proud to be the first in my family to attend college. I was on the fast-track to success.

But within the first month of school, I was failing not one but *two* classes.

I was enrolled in a level-four French class, after three years of language studies in high school, and found myself in way over my head. It was like the professor was speaking Japanese! I just couldn't keep up. My first-ever accounting class wasn't much better; the professor might have been speaking in Japanese, too, for all I knew. I didn't understand what that goofy man was trying to tell me about debits to the window and credits to the wall (and I certainly never envisioned a future as a CPA *at that point*). I channeled everything my parents had taught me and thought to myself, *If I'm patient, I'll figure this out.* But the more I tried to figure it out, the worse it got. The lessons kept building on each other, and I kept falling further behind. In this case, my "patience" wasn't paying off.

I finally approached my French professor, who of course insisted we call her Mademoiselle, to ask for some help. She was absolutely unforgiving. Her entire response came back to me in French, and she demanded I speak to her only in French—this was an advanced college-level class, after all. I stood there dumbfounded. How was I to move forward if I couldn't explain my problems to this woman and if she continued to speak a language I didn't understand?

I wasn't prepared for this, and my ego was loud and relentless: *You're worthless. You're letting yourself down. You can't speak a lick of French. You can't handle basic accounting stuff. You should quit.* I went on many long walks by myself during this time. I thought a lot. I asked myself some difficult questions: *Is it worth it? Should I start over? Get out? Become a car mechanic, perhaps?* I prayed about it as well, seeking some divine intervention.

And I almost dropped out.

FIRING THE EGO

I was caught in a twenty-foot tidal wave of rejection and worthlessness, and I had to dig down deep to find the part of me I knew was inside, the part of me that was a problem-solver, a fixer, an overcomer. This was something I had learned from my parents, who worked hard for everything we had. My parents didn't solve my problems for me—they empowered me to solve my own, to put the time in, and to not give up. For this reason, I didn't want to disappoint them, and this was a huge motivation for me during this time.

When I started diving into the muck, the first thing I encountered was my sense of entitlement. I thought I should be getting good grades, that the momentum that carried me through high school should sustain me through the rest of my education. Again, my ego speaking. And I was dead wrong. Feelings of entitlement are a dead end. They are the fantasy of a fool.

After I faced that head-on—after I acknowledged this false belief that I deserved some good grades that I hadn't yet earned—I heard a different voice rise up from the ashes: *You're giving up too early. You can figure this out.* There was another truer part of me having a debate with my ego. My inner self was saying that the consequences of failing were not as bad as the consequences of quitting. *And you'll know you quit for the rest of your life!*

And I realized: this wasn't my professors' problem, nor was it my parents', or my roommate's, or my girlfriend's three towns over. This was *my* problem, my challenge, and the only person I would ultimately be letting down by not solving it was—you guessed it—*me*.

If I quit, I was the one who would have to live with that decision every day of my life. If I quit, I would be giving up on myself. And that was far worse than failing a couple of classes. Moreover, quitting was in conflict with my self-esteem, another trait my parents instilled in me at a very young age. (And, in my opinion, the most important trait you can instill in your children when they are young, as it is a powerful driver for success.)

So my true self told my ego to bug off, leave me alone. I had to face the remorse and the lack of self-worth head-on in order to unlock these doors. I had to ask myself: what were my actual choices?

COMPARTMENTALIZING

I realized that the response my French professor gave me was a gift. She put my problem back into my own hands. She forced me to figure it out, to ask myself—in whatever language I understood (i.e., not French)—what I wanted and how to get that. And while she could have solved the problem for me, she didn't. She made me look in the mirror and consider what kind of person I was going to be. It was my choice.

So I left. That is, her class. I dropped down two levels in French, resigned myself to two more years of learning the language than I had originally anticipated, told my ego to hit the road, and did the work. This decision required a great deal of humility on my part. I had to admit that my high school experience in French hadn't actually prepared me for college as well as I had thought or expected. I had to admit that I didn't understand and that no amount of effort was going to magically download French words into my head overnight.

If we are true to ourselves, we need to pause occasionally and ask ourselves if we are really on the right track. Are we doing what is in our best interests and are we doing all we are capable of to succeed? If it's not working out, a course correction (no pun intended) is likely essential, and any feelings of humility or shame will be at odds with our ego, *but so what?* Make the course correction and move on. We're not here on Earth destined to have a miserable life. Our lives can be enriched by our experiences, our choices, and our faith that we can do better.

The next thing I had to recognize was that the problem in the French class was separate from the issues I was having in accounting. Failure is tricky like that. It puts your mind into a defeated place. Did I make a poor choice, or was I just not trying hard enough? I had let the failure in a language course spill over into an accounting course (and elsewhere). I needed to sort it all out. "Woe is me" would not fix anything.

Far too often, we compound things that have nothing to do with each other. My incompetency in French was unrelated to the struggles I was having in accounting, although I let these two separate issues build into an overall sense of defeat. I was in over my head in French; I needed to dial it back. The accounting class was a good choice—any career in business would require basic accounting fundamentals—so I needed to choose not just to get through it but to prove myself. I needed to dig deeper, and I needed another way of seeing things. I needed to check my perspective.

This is an important life skill, to be able to compartmentalize and decipher our problems in a way that doesn't become self-deprecating or all-encompassing. If my basement floods and a deal falls through on the same day, it might be easy to jump to the conclusion that I'm a failure (or that life is unfair). But in reality, these two mishaps have nothing to do with each other. And—likely—they aren't reflective of who I am, my capabilities, or my future. They are problems that can be solved, but one at a time, with different approaches and different considerations. Too often in these moments, we get caught up in a wave of emotion and let ourselves be beaten up by this. It's more difficult—but far more beneficial—to take a step back, have a conversation with yourself, and figure out how to overcome it.

The way to swim out of these waves of emotion is one stroke at a time. Try to break it all down into smaller pieces and focus on getting a few easy ones out of the way. The achievements will strengthen your spirit to take down the larger bits. Pretty soon, those feelings (and your ego) will start to diminish so that you can push through with determination, with a true belief that you are not destined to fail but to succeed and live a better, richer life because you're worth it and you deserve it.

HUMBLE PIE

Humility and humiliation are two different things. Humiliation is an emotional feeling—we feel ashamed we failed, we are embarrassed that we let ourselves and others down. In its worst form, humiliation causes us to feel unworthy, anxious, and depressed. In many cases, humiliation arises because we've set unreasonable expectations for ourselves, tried to be something we're not, or put too much weight on our outward appearance or accomplishments. My failing French did not reflect on my worthiness or overall competence as a human. This wasn't something to be *ashamed* of. It was simply a truth that I had to own and a problem I had to solve. Owning this took humility.

After solving the French problem, I met with my accounting professor, who thankfully spoke to me in English. He put me in touch with an older student who was willing to tutor me in accounting, who helped me start at the beginning and build a better foundation for understanding.

This godsend of a tutor began by explaining that debits to the window and credits to the wall was a metaphor, and that I had taken some of the professor's dry humor a bit too literally. Once he started explaining that there is symmetry in accounting, that things have to balance and reconcile, and that accounting was just a system of organizing and separating assets and liabilities from income and expenses, a light went on in my head. Suddenly I grasped it and went on to finish with a minor in accounting. Later in my life, I would take a master's program in taxation and pass the CPA exam. A powerful lesson for me to change the texture of the voice and my perceptions.

In all of this, I had to face my fear of failure. That was my elusive ego speaking. The ego is a funny thing. Most of us rarely think consciously about it. If we let it, it's capable of doing all sorts of things: lull us into a false sense of security, alter our identities, shame us when we fail, and heap all kinds of guilt upon us. Ego can also drive us toward unimaginable achievements and help us realize capabilities we didn't know we had. It can both pull and push us in multiple directions.

There is a saying about our need to "keep our egos in check." I believe this is true and that keeping our egos in check—meaning, recognizing how much power we give it—requires a conscious and consistent effort in acknowledgment and confrontation. Our goal in life should not just be achievement and presenting a respectable face to the world. We are all on a journey to knowing ourselves—our true selves—and offering this beauty (and brokenness!) to the people around us. We have to shed the ego in order to grow, in order to be honest and real. Shedding the ego for a while is healthy and enables us to see ourselves for who and what we really are, to be honest with ourselves, and to carefully examine our real needs at any point in time.

Humility is the absence of arrogance and pride, laying aside entitlement and the "I deserve this" attitude. Humility is also a conscious state of mind, recognizing that we are equals with everyone but that no two people walk the same path in life. Each is different and unique. We're not better than anyone, but we're not worse, and we all have a right to be happy and successful in this life. If we can embrace our mistakes, accept them as our teachers, and move on, we can self-heal and restore our feeling of being worthy but not prideful or indulgent. Humility is a powerful companion.

PASSING THROUGH

This is a story that repeats itself several times in my life. It was perhaps the first moment I realized that I was passing through, that my experiences in college—my successes and my failures—were paving the way for the next thing. And the passing-through part was essential. There wasn't an option to bypass the journey. That would compromise the next thing I wanted to do. The passing through enabled me to move to the next milestone and then the next and then the next one after that. I had to move through these problems, face the possibility of failure, and work it out in order to move forward.

This is the question I have asked myself throughout my life and career: *am I on the right path?* When I make decisions, I try to think about how I'll feel about the decision tomorrow. Or the day after. Or three years from now. Whether it was choosing a college (or considering dropping out), pursuing a particular relationship, staying in a job, saying yes to an opportunity—I would ask myself, *How do you feel about that choice now? And how do you think you'll feel about it later?*

Is it going to help you get where you want to go?

Life is a series of steps, hopefully reflecting the choices we've made. This is how the journey becomes the destination. Each step forward is a prequel to the next. There is no right or wrong sequence, as long as they are your chosen steps.

Dropping out of college would mark me a failure that I couldn't afford for the rest of my life. I would have been quitting on far more than a few years of education. I would have been quitting on my hopes for the future: my dreams, opportunities, and paving my own way. And quitting is contagious; it's a downward spiral. We quit one thing and it gives us permission to quit so many more. And at the end of the day, the person we let down most often and most profoundly is ourselves. I felt this in the depths of me—if I walk out on this, what else would I be willing to walk out on?

Sticking around also wasn't a sure path to success. Hiring a tutor and demoting myself in French was hardly a guarantee that I would pass with flying colors. However, it was a deeper commitment to the process, an acknowledgment that I was in it for the long haul, a rally cry—I wasn't giving up on myself that easily. This was a proving ground.

College wasn't easy for me. It did get a whole lot easier once I realized I could make better choices for myself, that—if I truly applied myself and put the effort in—I could get through any course (that I was qualified to be in). With a focus on why I was there and that I was just passing through, I empowered myself to think beyond the college experience and to what I would do next. Not only did this open doors for me to achieve more, but I also became happier and more self-confident.

I graduated from Augsburg College in 1972, with honors and degrees in finance and economics. I was ready to take on the world. Back then, career choices were thought to be forever. Most people didn't ever change jobs like they do so often today, so the importance of making the right choice was a heavy burden. What was I going to do?

My dad advised me to take a safe and secure job with a stable employer. "Maybe a position with the US Postal Service would be to your liking, son? You can handle that," he told me. I was mortified at the idea of a life I pictured as mundane and repetitive. I explained to my dad that, while the risk of my failure in a business enterprise might be higher than the risk of starting in a governmental clerk position and working my way up, I thought the opportunities were greater in business. I actually felt it, and I believed it. I was certain of it.

I also realized that it was likely going to be incredibly challenging for me, as most everything worthwhile in my life has been. My dad was honest. He spoke from a reference point he was familiar with. He also knew I wanted to set a greater expectation of myself, for which he became my advocate. No matter what, my folks were always there, and above all else, they loved me no matter what. Ultimately, they let me live my life and live with my choices.

A KEY: FAILURE

Question: Are you willing to fire your ego and get real?

I was failing French and clearly in over my head. I was also doing poorly in basic accounting, but for different reasons. Both problems were addressable, but not until I could accept that those were *my* problems.

I had a choice: to drop out, to take an F, or to find a solution to overcome. Deep down, I knew success would feel better than failure. I just had to decide that I was worth the effort it would take. I had to declare it out loud: I had a right to be happy and successful. I could figure it out and it would be worth the effort.

It's easy to get caught up in emotions, to listen to the voice inside your head that tells you that you're a failure, a disappointment, a waste. Don't be deceived. This is not humility. This is your ego protecting you, convincing you that taking a risk, asking for help, or changing directions altogether is foolish. This is your ego trying to get you to play it safer next time, to internalize your feelings, and to do whatever it takes to save face.

The truth is, if we cling to the edge of the pool all day long and never get out into the deep end and learn to swim, we will never experience life. But this doesn't come without risk and ultimately—*inevitably*—without failure. Some people let the fear of failure get the best of them, and they never learn how to swim. Or they keep one hand anchored to the edge of the pool, never testing their limits and realizing their fullest potential. However, the more we learn how to swim, the more creative we become, the more we see and experience, and the less we rely on the edge.

Failure is a gift, if we allow it to be. We have more to learn from our mistakes than any of our successes. But this posture requires humility and grace: accepting the truth that we will never be perfect and that we are on a journey of continuous growth. One of life's greatest gifts is that we don't know everything, that we haven't learned certain things yet, that we can always change and become better.

We therefore have to embrace the benefits and opportunities that come from mistakes—we have to accept these situations as what they are: the very best teachers. Your professors, your friends, your teachers, your mentors, your pastors—they can't teach you what failure can. It's a deeply personal experience that affects your mind, emotions, and self-esteem.

While failure is a natural part of life, it's brutal for your ego. Your hurt ego can and will hold you down and make you feel ashamed and unworthy. You'll stay down until you release your ego, recognizing that this manifestation is not the truest version of yourself. You may need to consciously proclaim it, speak it out loud: "I'm moving on"; "I'm better for having survived this mistake"; "I'm a stronger person now." The most honest version of yourself is probably not the infallible, overly confident, invincible person that your ego projects.

Chapter 3

WHAT IF I DON'T WANT TO BE AN ADMIRAL?

DURING COLLEGE, I was fortunate to have started working part-time at a bank as a teller, among other things. Now, there are tellers inside the bank, and there are also tellers at the drive-up where people can make deposits without having to get out of their cars (I think this is still a thing today). On this particular day in April, I had shown up to work ready to take my position behind the teller counter, when my supervisor told me I would be working the drive-up window that day.

No problem, I thought. *Easy peasy.*

He gave me a quick rundown on the logistics: There are five lanes, five rows of cars, and two tellers to handle these lanes. One teller oversees lanes one and two; the other teller, lanes three through five. The first lane is the real, live person, behind bulletproof glass (the one that used to give your kids lollipops). The rest of the lanes do business through pneumatic tubes.

"Greg," he said, "you're going to be working lanes three through five."

"Alrighty, got it," I said.

"Here's your machine. Here's how you post debits and credits, just like the tele-window, except now you have a TV monitor and three pneumatic tubes that'll be coming in."

"Are the tubes numbered to match the lanes?" I asked.

"No," the bossman replied. "The lanes are numbered. The tubes are colored. The orange tube is lane three, red is four, and green is five."

And before I knew it, he patted me on the back and off he went. Now, it was Friday at four o'clock in the afternoon. It was a month-end payday for most people and social security day. It was also the beginning of a three-day federal holiday. There were cars lined up: five across, ten deep. That's fifty automobiles, in case you didn't do the math. I didn't have time to think things over; I got right to work thinking, *I got this*. The tubes started coming up, I posted the transactions, and I sent the tubes back on their merry way with deposit receipts, cash, whatever. In the rush, I didn't look up. But apparently, if I had, I would have seen people getting out of their cars to swap tubes, and it wasn't long before a few of them were inside the building, giving the bank officers an earful. I was sending the wrong tubes to the wrong cars. It was absolute pandemonium out there!

Now, it would have been easy for the bank officers to write me off as a total incompetent idiot. But by this point, I had worked at the bank for over a year and had done nothing but prove myself the opposite. I was competent and motivated and a pleasure to work with, if I do say so myself. We were all dumbfounded. And of course, I felt horrible. I felt worse than horrible because I had let everyone around me down, no matter that it was totally unintentional. Even though no one thought for a minute that I had willingly mixed up the tubes, I couldn't have felt worse.

Thankfully, they all paused, and one of the bank officers asked me what was going on. Why was I sending the green tube down the orange slot? I was honest: all of the colors looked the same to me. There was no green or orange or red.

You could ask me what I saw when I was looking at those tubes, and it would be impossible to explain. I could guess that the tube was green, but it would have only been a guess. And clearly, I wasn't guessing right! I wasn't really aware that I was color-blind up to this point, but I knew as soon as I was holding all three of those tubes that there were going to be some problems.

Thankfully, they paused long enough to uncover the underlying problem, and someone was intuitive enough to ask what was going on. And it was a quick fix. We added the lane numbers to the corresponding tubes, and I was back at it, minus the chaos.

Thinking back on this, it would have taken only one bank officer or one irate customer to demand that I be fired on the spot. So, yes, I would have felt worse than I already did. It would have been easy for the bank to explain to the customers that they fired the fool at the drive-up teller cameras. But one person was willing to ask how this happened and to give me a break. She understood there had to be a reason. Rather than pitch me out, she fixed the problem, and with ease: a little duct tape and a black magic marker.

It's also interesting to note the powerful impact this could have had on my life. If that bank manager hadn't stepped in to uncover my color blindness, I don't know when I would have discovered it. It's really amazing I made it that far in life without it causing other mix-ups. Or maybe it had and I didn't know it. Maybe I was lucky to be alive! If they had fired me, I may have never worked in a bank again. I likely would have chosen some other vocation, and only God knows where I'd be today or what I would have accomplished with my life. As it turned out, that one act of kindness enabled me to get right back on the horse and—years later—be successfully involved in dozens of bank acquisitions and mergers all over the country.

FINDING THE REAL PROBLEM

Much to my dismay, my now eleven-year-old grandson inherited this unfortunate color-blind trait, and also found this out the hard way. He's a very skilled hockey player, goes to a full-time hockey school, and scores more goals per capita than any other player on his teams. I mean, he's being trained like the Russians and Chinese train their national athletes. It's intense. And he's very, very good. (And he is also quite charming if I may say so, and I guess I just did.)

A couple of years ago, he was on the ice, in the middle of a game, wearing a black jersey, while the other team was sporting burgundy. The game started and my grandson, Cooper, scored the first goal… for the other team. He returned to his team's bench and his coach asked, "Why did you do that?"

That's when Cooper realized he had scored for the wrong team. He panicked a little bit and said, "Coach, I don't know! I can't see!"

And his coach went into a frenzy. "What happened? Are you alright? Are you injured? How many fingers am I holding up?"

Cooper said, "One."

"Were you hit in the head?" his coach asked.

"No, but I can't see. I scored for the other team."

"I know, but...*why*?"

And Cooper finally said, "I can't tell what color they're wearing. I'm confused."

Again, it's easy to jump to conclusions in these high-stress moments. An eleven-year-old's hockey game isn't life or death, but had the coach continued to assume that Cooper was seriously injured, instead of digging in and asking one of the most important questions —WHY—this whole ordeal could have gotten way out of hand. And again, another simple solution: now his coach carries ten white jerseys and ten black jerseys in his bag to every game, so Cooper can always decipher who his team is on the ice.

Cooper's coach and my supervisor at the bank ultimately helped us to know something important about ourselves. There was stress and confusion but certainly not a life crisis. Knowing ourselves and knowing about ourselves is critical in making the best choices later in our lives. Sometimes we can ultimately figure these things out ourselves, but sometimes it takes someone else pausing just long enough to take interest and help us on the way. They see a problem and they see a way to fix it.

Our lives are filled with problems and challenges far greater than color blindness. You see them every day. When you see someone challenged or suffering with a problem and you can see a fix or a better alternative, will you speak up or walk on? A small gesture of kindness, which may seem inconsequential at the time, could be life-altering for someone. The point is, we can all look at the same problem and draw a number of different conclusions. But when we are too quick to assume, we can miss out on quick fixes and great team members.

WILLING TO WORK

Despite the drive-up window incident, upon graduating from college, the bank offered me a spot in a training program. The premise of the program was that I would work in all of the departments of the bank—marketing, HR, new accounts, commercial lending, mortgages—shadowing all kinds of people and completing a variety of assignments. It was intended to be a two-year program, but I was doing so well that ten months in, they offered me a full-time job as a credit analyst. I was thrilled! Coincidentally, they placed me at their new starship bank, which had just been built in Bloomington, Minnesota, where I grew up.

They told me that there was nobody doing the credit analysis work, that they were backed up and needed someone who could figure out the financials for all of the commercial business customers that borrowed money from the bank. This included car dealers, landscapers, insurance and real estate agents, physicians, dentists, and so on. Their financial statements and tax returns were rolling in, and they needed someone to analyze them. This person would work directly with the business owners' financial officers to sort all of this information out in order to get the credits ready for loan approval by the board of directors.

I said, "OK, I can do that." And that's how I got started in banking.

There were seven commercial loan officers that I worked under at the time, and this was kind of like working inside seven different banks. They each had different expectations and needs, but—across the board, one thing was clear—none of them were going to do the "grunt work" that was assigned to me. I was to do whatever they needed me to do, and I was grateful to do it. It was an incredible opportunity to progress from being a part-time teller to a full-time credit analyst, and I quit thinking about joining the postal service.

I knew that this job was a stepping stone in my journey. I knew it when I was locking up the bank by myself at midnight. I knew it when I was driving in to work at the crack of dawn, and when I was chasing down impossible information, and when I was filing paperwork and reading endless finance jargon. This was a step to perhaps becoming an officer of the bank—maybe even a president someday!—and I thought that sounded like a worthy, fascinating career path at the time.

The more time I put in, the more experience I had under my belt, the less sharpened my single focus was on becoming a commercial loan officer in a bank. I started to see my life like a tree, with many branches. The roots were my past—my upbringing, my work ethic, my education. The trunk was my confidence in myself, my openness to possibilities. And the branches were all of these options that could open up. I had found a way to nurture these things, they were thriving, and I was excited about the future. Surely my hard work would result in promotion and advancement, I thought.

Now, mind you, this was 1972 and there were no computers. We had typewriters and magical carbon paper so we could make two copies of something. We relied on the US Postal Service to get what we needed from clients. There was no such thing as the internet or Google, so when I was tasked to learn about funeral homes or a client's construction project that needed an $18 million line of credit, I walked my butt to the library to read a good-ole-fashioned book or industry guide. And I was going to the library a lot those days to learn about different subjects and trades, to locate documentation, and to find out how to measure different financial statement metrics and ratios.

Once again, I found innovation was my friend. I couldn't run around asking busy people how to do my job; I had to get creative and figure it out myself. These were my problems and I had to own them. I might not have been the smartest person in the room—OK, I definitely wasn't the smartest person in the room—but I wasn't afraid to do the work. I was clear on my position: at the bottom of the totem pole. And I was clear on my job: to do the bidding of seven different loan officers.

SERVANTHOOD

Four years down the road, still a credit analyst, I realized that I had become a crutch for these seven lenders. One was named Jake, one was named Dick, and one was named Bill. Jake was demanding, Bill was a jerk, and Dick "needed his stuff yesterday," but I had four other loan officers to deal with. I was their Google, their digital boy when there was no digital world. They could call on me for anything and I was forced to figure it out, research it, and create it. I felt like I was on a hamster wheel. Where was my promotion?

Initially, I had thought becoming a lender would be great. While still in the analyst role, after hiring and training another couple of analysts who worked for me, I even got to do some lending myself. But these seven lenders were protective of their fiefdom; they didn't want me to become a lender because I'd start working on the same accounts; I'd start bringing in new customers to the bank; I would be their competition, and they didn't want their digital boy competing with them.

Furthermore, in my little bit of experience with commercial lending at the time, I didn't find it as rewarding as I had expected. I would look at a business, at its financials, and I could see that the customer maybe deserved a credit. But then I'd look past the credit at his business and think, *Boy, this business could be a lot better if they just did this.* Or, *This business could make a lot more money if they implemented that.* The trouble was, that was not the role of the bank. Banks don't give advice; it may conflict with making the loan.

I had vision—I could see a way for businesses to be more profitable based on their financial statements. I really wanted to tell them how they could do better at what they were doing. But I wasn't a CPA. I wasn't a finance wizard. I didn't come out of the Wharton School of business and economics. Yes, I had a degree in finance and economics, but I didn't have any credentials and I could barely look up. I was working sixteen-hour days, had a wife and a child, and had just bought a house one block away from the bank. How could I give that all up?

I felt stuck.

THE SURE PATH

I had to reevaluate. Was the objective I was working toward going to make me happy? It was a programmed career, a sure pathway in the industry. I would eventually migrate to the next position, to the next desk, then to a bigger desk, then a cubicle, then a small office, then a bigger office, and if I was incredibly lucky, I would maybe become a bank president someday. It was like being in the military. You start out at the bottom and you work your way up to a two-star captain, a three-star commander, until finally you're an admiral. And I had to be honest with myself: *what if I don't want to be an admiral?*

Maybe there was something else in this "navy" that I would like to do. Maybe there were different shoes for me to fill. Suddenly, I couldn't see the planned pathway in the bank as the way to finding myself challenged, rewarded, and happy. And these were things I valued far more than a safe, sure path.

Even though I was now seven years out of college, and hardly wanted to restart my career, I knew the quickest way to change things up, retool, and begin again was to get the hell out of that bank and do away with the analyst title that seemed to define and limit me.

A KEY: SELF-INSPECTION

Question: How's that working for you?

I had many factors to consider when I was making the decision to pivot to a new career path, and asking myself the difficult questions was part of the process. How would my parents respond (after all, they expected me to pick a career and stick with it)? What impact would this have on my pregnant wife, our mortgage, our car payment, and our lifestyle? Did I have the time to start over? Furthermore, could I really do something else? If the goal was to become a CPA, was I capable? (That rough start in my college accounting class wasn't *that* far behind me.)

Whether you're considering a big change or choosing to stay put, self-inspection is a valuable practice. You will never know what you are living for and what you *want* to be living for unless you're willing to ask. And the only person who knows these answers is yourself.

Are you on the right path? Are you happy? What makes you happy? Prestige? Wealth? Helping others? What do you expect of yourself? How do you hold yourself accountable?

It was only in asking myself these types of questions that I was able to identify that if I stayed in the bank, I was settling for more of the same. They didn't want to promote me. I didn't want to be a loan officer. What I really wanted to do (advise people in business, point them in the right direction) wasn't an option at the bank. But the path ahead required my fullest, most undivided commitment. It wouldn't be easy (most things worthy of our time are not), and I would have to endure some grinding years, but I was pretty certain—after a process of self-inspection—that I couldn't keep doing what I was doing and that the path toward fulfillment required a total restart.

Maybe your self-inspection is as simple as asking, "How's this working for me?" Whether you're talking about a job, a relationship, a lifestyle, you name it, don't be afraid to ask yourself the difficult questions. The worst thing you are going to discover is that you are unhappy (and in reality, you already knew that, whether you admitted it or not). You can't pursue positive change until you've been honest with yourself. You know how you feel, and you will always know if you did something about it.

The next step is finding out what you can do about it, how you can initiate the beginning of change and find a path forward toward a solution. I recognize that many people do not have the luxury of shifting careers midway through their life. The cost is too great, to themselves or their family or their future. But are you truly stuck? Is there something that you can do to make the situation better? To grow as a person, either professionally or personally? To make life more enjoyable? To take care of yourself? The solution does not have to be as dramatic as starting all over as a CPA. But you have to believe that the solution is inside of you and finding it begins with asking yourself the right questions.

There's no better time than right now to take a look at yourself and at your life and decide what needs to give. Does that mean you have to do it every minute of every day? Absolutely not. But don't wait until you're ten or twenty years down the road in an endeavor to seek deeper, meaningful answers. There is still time. And you most assuredly are worth it!

Chapter 4

HAVE YOU LOST YOUR MIND?

I LIKED EXAMINING BUSINESSES and giving financial advice. That was one of my biggest takeaways from my time at the bank. I liked it, and I was good at it. I realized that if I were going to give business advice in that day and age, having a CPA license was the golden ticket. It was an essential credential to have.

However, the only way to unwrap this golden ticket was to obtain the two years of required experience at a CPA firm. And the only way to get these two years of experience was to get hired by a CPA firm. So I went out and interviewed with some of the big guns—Price Waterhouse, Ernst & Whinney, Coopers & Lybrand—and it was a complete waste of time. They would never hire a twenty-eight-year-old with no CPA license or prior accounting experience. They would only hire kids straight out of college that had accounting degrees, had a 4.0 GPA, and had already sat for the CPA.

Now Northwest Bank, my place of employment at the time, was located in a big, beautiful building on the HY 494 strip in Minneapolis—right around the corner from where the Minnesota

Vikings and the Twins played. While the bank occupied the first three floors of this tower, above it were all sorts of businesses and professionals: lawyers, accountants, insurance companies, advisors, HQs for various companies. These folks had to pass through the lobby of our bank, where I sat at my desk and greeted them each morning (no big shot office for analyst/junior lender!).

Halfway up the building, on the eighth floor, was a small CPA firm with about eight partners. Some of the businesses at the bank used this firm for their audits and tax returns, so I knew several of the partners, but I didn't yet know the head honcho, the Managing Partner. I did know a few things about him, however: this quiet man stood all of five foot one, was highly revered, and threw an infamous pool party in his backyard every summer. We had crossed paths (meaning, he had crossed mine on his way up to the eighth floor), and I thought he might know who I was.

One morning, it dawned on me that there was a potential opportunity right there, in front of my nose. Maybe I meant nothing to these enormous, hoity-toity firms, but this small CPA firm wasn't one of these firms. A small firm like this was concerned about survival, and the only way to survive is to get more clients. And here I was—after four years at the bank—with a list of potential clients in my head. I might be just what they were looking for.

I decided to head up to the eighth floor to see if I could schedule a meeting with the Managing Partner to discuss a future in accounting (or at least get the two-year experience requirement out of the way). I didn't have an appointment that day, but I approached the receptionist with a smile, inquired about her morning, and asked if I could see the boss.

"Who are you?" she asked.

"I'm Greg Smith from the bank," I replied.

"What do you do at the bank?"

I said, "Well, I'm an analyst. Tell him it's Greg Smith from the bank. He knows who I am."

And sure enough (much to my surprise), she came back and said, "He'll see you now."

I couldn't believe it. This was a one-shot opportunity. I wasn't even sure what I was going to talk to him about. I was twenty-eight years old, with no accounting experience of any kind, and was pretty certain that if I came in and asked for a job, there wasn't a chance I'd actually get one. But I have always been drawn to possibilities. Maybe, even more so, long shots. And this was most definitely one of those.

I told him that I worked at the bank downstairs, where his firm kept all of their money and many of their partners did their banking, and that I just wanted to pick his brain about something—sort of an informational interview, if you will.

A voice in my left ear was saying, *Fool, get out of here. Get back to your desk and preserve your chosen vocation. Think of your wife, your mortgage, your daughter. And by God, what will your parents say?*

But the louder voice in my other ear was saying, *Be cool. Be a mature executive looking for an opportunity. You know so many business owners. You can bring in piles of business to this firm and this guy will get that. You're the only one that knows about your horrible grades in accounting college courses!* I decided to listen to this voice.

He asked me how I liked my job as an analyst.

"Well, I don't like it as much as I thought I would," I said, honestly. "And I'm thinking that if I'm going to be successful, I should have some better credentials. I don't have an accounting degree, but I'm willing to get one so that I can take the CPA exam. And I will study for the CPA exam and I promise you, I will pass it, by hook or crook." (In hindsight, crook may not have been the best verb choice since there is an "ethics" part of the exam.)

He said, "Where do you live?"

"Ummm, actually I live right down there," I said, pointing out his big window, where we could see my house a block away through the trees.

"How old are you?" he asked.

This conversation was taking a rather strange turn.

"I'm twenty-eight," I said.

"Are you married?"

"Yep. That's my wife down there watering the grass," I said.

"Do you have children?"

"Yes, sir. I have a one-year-old daughter named Lindsay."

He said, "Well, have you lost your mind?"

Uh oh.

I took a chance and said, "Look, I know I'm an unlikely candidate, but let me tell you what I can do for you. I know every business that walks in and out of that bank downstairs. I know their financials, their peer groups, their profit margins, and I know them because I analyze their credits. Here's the thing: if they're not audit or tax clients of your firm, they should be because they've got shit for accountants and nobody does the kind of work that your firm does. You've got great partners, a great reputation. You're a great firm all around. There are all these crummy little wannabe CPA firms that are putting up financial statements. I've seen them and they do miserable work, and worse—they don't advise their clients on what to do and how to improve, and the bank can't do it because it's too big of a conflict. But this is something I can do. I may not be a CPA, but I will be one, and I know how to help small businesses improve."

He looked me in the eyes and without missing a beat, he said, "When do you want to start?"

I said, "How about in two weeks?"

He shook my hand, told me I was hired, and that was that.

I took the elevator back down to my desk job at the bank. That evening, I spoke to my wife and—after hearing me out—she smiled and said she was 100 percent on board and supportive. She knew I was feeling stifled and unhappy at the bank. She could tell I was expressing my true feelings and conviction about the move and the work ahead.

But we were both absolutely stunned that I was hired on the spot. Nothing in my life has ever come easy. I have had to plan and work diligently, with great focus, to get most anything done. The notion to seek employment with this small (but conveniently located) CPA firm had just come to me, like one of those cartoon-lightbulbs-over-the-head moments. Most importantly, it felt right.

Now, I didn't know if the Managing Partner was going to put me in the tax department, the audit department, or the consulting department—heck, I didn't care. As long as I was out of that bank, I was moving up in the world—eight stories, to be exact—and I was going to reset my expectations, my obligations, and my commitments. And, of course, I was going to restart my entire career and head back to school.

PLAY YOUR CARDS RIGHT

I struck out at the big CPA firms because I would never be what they were looking for. There was no way around it—I was too old, my GPA too low, my CPA license nonexistent. I didn't have anything to offer these national firms, not even an accounting degree. I could have let that defeat me, send me running with my tail between my legs.

But then I realized that there was an opportunity right there in front of me. And I also realized that I wasn't going to get very far without offering something in return: you hire me, here's what I can give you. I had something they needed—access to more clients. I didn't have *all* of what they needed, but I had something, and I believed—at the very depths of my being—that I could help them get to where they needed to go. These were the cards in my back pocket, and I played them with as much confidence as I could muster. It may have been a pair of sixes, but I played it like a full house.

You see, figuring out your cards is only half the battle. The other half is believing you can do something with them. If you don't believe you can do it, why should anyone else believe it? Once you realize you have some cards, you can't just *hope* to play them successfully. You have to play them with conviction, with faith. You have to play them like you know you're going to win the pot.

I often reference having "hope" versus having "faith." For me, hope and faith are very different. Hope refers to something I might wish for. Hope sets an expectation that something may come true, but this outcome depends on the facts and circumstances around it. And self confidence!

Faith is an inner belief that my actions can positively affect an outcome. If I don't give up, if I do all that I can, this *will* happen.

But true faith requires a belief in a higher power. (I defer to you to define what that higher power might be in your life, and I hope for your sake you have one.) My personal reference is to God. My belief is that most of us can move through the unique challenges of our lives by calling upon a higher power for inspiration and upon our inner selves for answers to difficult questions. This is where we find deep, unwavering belief in what we can and will accomplish.

DEDICATION

I gave my notice to the bank (they weren't surprised), and despite their pleas for me to stick around and promises to soon make me a loan officer, I stayed true to myself. The work wasn't interesting to me. I had hit a dead end, and I needed to add more branches to my tree. A few of the senior bank executives offered their best wishes for me and encouraged me to stay in touch. Several assured me that this was the right decision. One even said privately that he wished he had made a move like this when he was younger. Interesting. With my eye on the prize—a CPA license and therefore a passport to a real executive job—I took a humiliating salary reduction and started my gig as a staff accountant in the audit department of this small firm.

Day one with my new boss, Alan, the partner in charge of audits, was an absolute disaster. Alan had just returned to the office that same day, after two weeks in the sun. And by two weeks in the sun, I mean he was bright red and visibly uncomfortable. As the audit partner for the firm, Alan was responsible for 70 percent of the billing and staff and had single-handedly hired his entire team. Upon arriving at work that day, he had no idea that the Managing Partner had hired me and assigned me to his team while he was basking in the Caribbean sun. This fact was obvious when he stormed out of his boss's office with a slam of the door and his already sun-scorched face a tad redder.

He beelined it to my cubicle where I was already helping one of the other staff accountants with a project. Towering over me at six foot six, Alan told me to get up. He then grabbed my elbow with a vice grip (it still hurts to think about it) and marched me around to fifteen other employees on his audit team, all fresh-out-of-college recruits and about seven years my junior.

"New recruit!" Alan bellowed. "This is Smith. He is here to be of service to you all. Need paper supplies? Pencils sharpened? (No, we still did not have computers at this time.) Lunch delivery? Tell Smith! That's his job. It's what he's qualified to do."

He hadn't hired me and he was pissed, and he sure as heck wanted everyone to know it.

Now, Alan's physical presence was intimidating. His eyes bugged out and a vein or two were protruding from his temples. I noticed right away that his nose had been broken in several places, which suggested to me that he might like to get into a fight or two. (I later learned he used to box.) At the end of my morning office tour with Alan, I was honestly just grateful I hadn't been tossed out the twelfth-floor window into my backyard (back when the office windows still opened). And by the end of the day, I was sincerely regretting leaving the safety of the promising career track at the bank.

However, during my first week at the firm, nearly everyone stopped by to offer encouragement and to fill me in on Alan's reputation for blowing up over small matters and occasionally overlooking really important ones. Sure, he was a bully, but he was also my boss and I had to figure out how to deal with him, since there wasn't another CPA firm in the Twin Cities that would hire me. Not the sharpest tool in the shed, Alan made up for his lack of intelligence with an extra dose of intimidation. And the truth was, Alan's ego was running the show. Alan's ego was the one showing up to work every day. The real Alan? I don't think I ever met him.

This intel enabled me to approach Alan differently. Some people begin to believe their own bullshit so much (in other words, their ego has so thoroughly convinced them that they are someone they're not) that there is no appealing to the deeper soul inside. In this case, I simply had to play to Alan's ego a bit. Actually, a lot. Thankfully, there was a visible expiration date on my business calendar. I could count each day of the next twenty-four months and then I would be out of there. In the meantime, for those 730 days, I could play the part of Alan's lowly assistant. I could fetch him coffees and call him sir and disconnect my greater self-worth and pride from those interactions. I knew, deep down, that I could succeed in this role and that it was a ticket to the next stop. I just had to choose not to be defeated by humiliation and this guy's personal vendetta against me.

SELF-RESPECT

I brought in a lot of new business to the firm, but I had neglected to negotiate a commission with the boss in our original conversation, and the barter I had made was done. I would never forget this mistake—in life, you get what you negotiate, not what's fair. I didn't think much of it at the time as our quid pro quo was a new job and a place to get the required two years of work experience for the CPA certification I had my eye on. I wanted to underpromise and overdeliver.

Once new businesses came in and word got around, even the bankers on the first floor were sending up clients to engage my firm as their auditors and tax preparers. Partners shared in the profits, not the lowly staff. More business in the firm meant more profit, and Alan was one of those beneficiaries. Plus, since most of the work I brought in was audit work, Alan was able to grow his department with more auditors and promote his staff to progress in the firm as seniors, supervising seniors, managers, and—for a few—partners. Over time, as the partners shared the profits, Alan began to back off. He even began to respect me, I think. I had unlocked the door to building a relationship with Alan or, at the very least, an understanding.

But that didn't stop him from assigning me the worst of the worst jobs. And—as the newest auditor—I had little leverage to avoid these inconvenient and sometimes impossible projects. Some of these included situations like the following:

- The client's CFO just quit; go out there and be the interim CFO.
- These financial records are an absolute mess; clean them up.
- This client just merged with another company; develop an integration plan.
- This client is under investigation by the IRS; find the necessary documentation and don't make it worse.
- We have a last-minute job that requires inhuman hours; hey, Greg, you only work 7:00 a.m. to 7:00 p.m., what about the other half of your day?

One of the most miserable jobs took place near Flint, Michigan (sometimes referred to as the proverbial butthole of the world), where I was dispatched multiple times to audit a social service agency that awarded grants to unemployed auto workers and their families. These families were nearly destitute. For generations, these families had been dependent on factory jobs at the car companies, which were frequently shuttered due to strikes or swings in the economy. At that time, interest rates were high and climbing higher, eventually topping off at over 21 percent. The federal and state agencies made it almost impossible for these families to receive essential aid due to ever-changing qualifications and tons of paperwork. We were there to audit the receipts and disbursements of these agencies, but looking past the numbers, we saw the sadness and grief of suffering people. These were innocent casualties of a fickle union and a constricted economy. It was heartbreaking.

Another challenging job was the audit of a regional auto parts store. Though I was running the job with crews at multiple locations, I was right in there with the staff, counting mufflers, tires, and other car components on New Year's Eve, through the night, into New Year's Day, because the stores were closed to retail traffic during this time and this was their year-end. Talk about a cruddy way to ring in the New Year!

I had to check my perspective constantly during my two years with this firm. Particularly every Saturday morning for six months, when I would drive across town to a dumpy, mouse-ridden industrial building and take my place behind a folding table on a rusted-out aluminum chair to spend eight hours learning how to pass the CPA exam (not to be confused with acquiring actual accounting skills).

This was a means to an end, another door to walk through that would lead to many other doors, many other possibilities. I simply had to endure and have faith that I would get through it.

It was a season of humility: taking my place at the very bottom, swallowing my pride, and working long, endless hours. I came across many arrogant people during this time—people who thought their positions in life justified unkindness, people who stepped on others on their upward climb, people who took advantage of their situations with dishonesty and disregard. These same people seemed to believe that their arrogance was the key to success, to wealth, and to respect. However, I have seen firsthand how arrogance leaves a path of destruction along its way and how—beneath the surface—it is actually a sign of deep insecurity, the exact opposite of self-respect.

I'm thankful for my years both at the bank and that little CPA firm, as they taught me that self-respect has very little to do with a job title, credentials, or a salary. I was proud of the person I was becoming and the hard work I continued to put in. I was proud of the risks I took and the family I had helped create and the relationships I had built over the years. I respected my goals, the process, and the people that helped me get to where I was. I respected my position at the bottom and all that I had yet to learn. I was honest with myself and I remained goal-centered. I could feel this was all going to be worth it.

A KEY: PERSEVERANCE

Question: What will it take to get there?

After two years of drudgery at a small firm, I passed the CPA exam, a true testament to how far I'd come from failing my first college accounting class. On the day I gave my notice, Alan came to my cubicle and demanded that I stand up. I thought, *Not this again.* And yep—we had indeed come full circle. He grabbed me by that same elbow with that same vice grip and marched me around to everyone, including partners, hollering out to anyone who would listen, "Smith is a rat fink! He is bailing out! A no-good quitter!" I couldn't tell if he was jesting or genuinely upset, so I tried to explain that I had accepted a position with a prominent banking family and was simply progressing my career, that it wasn't personal. This just made him more angry, to the point that he turned that same shade of sun-scorched red, stormed off, and slammed the door to his office. I never saw him again.

I made it through the two years with this bully of a boss and horrendous job assignments because I had a defined goal, a deeper purpose, a higher calling. Goals are incredible motivators, particularly if you can not only sense them but visualize how you will achieve them. It's impossible to know all of the challenges and obstacles you'll face. But it is possible to understand the importance and purpose of your goals and why they matter to you. What makes it a worthy goal? What are you willing to sacrifice to achieve it? What will you put up with?

I encountered a real-life monster, carrying a dark cloud of negativity and hate wherever he went, who intentionally tried to shame and defeat me. I had to rise above this toxic daily environment to keep my sight on the prize and not succumb to animosity. This experience was an invaluable teacher for me. It showed me what *not* to be. It bolstered my self-worth and my self-confidence. It taught me perseverance.

The type of perseverance that unlocks doors is sticking with something, even in the face of the most bleak odds. It involves fixing your eyes on a goal, so much so that it defines your purpose in being, regardless of how difficult the path to get there becomes. The achievement becomes personal to you—you can see it, taste it, feel it. You migrate from hoping or thinking about it to truly believing that it will get done. You'll tolerate most anything within a reasonable timeframe to achieve this kind of goal. Then, the experience and accomplishment will empower you and inform how you approach the next goal and the one after that.

Truly chasing your goals and dreams requires an unwavering commitment to yourself. You are worth the effort, the time, the energy, and the cost. You deserve your own attention and devotion. Even if your entire family thinks you're crazy, even if the decision doesn't make sense on paper, even if the financial setbacks seem daunting, your happiness is worth the cost. But you have to know what you're working toward and why, and then commit to it fully.

As you live through the unexpected challenges, as you commit to the sacrifices and own the decisions, you grow, learn, and become. But when the going gets tough, you have to believe in better days. You have to choose to persevere, believing that, in the end, the achievement will be worth the struggle. And that the achievement itself is just another door to pass through to the next great thing on your life's journey.

Chapter 5

WAIT FOR IT

I WAS THIRTY-ONE YEARS OLD when my two-year commitment at the CPA firm was coming to an end. I was more than ready for a change of scenery. In addition to my eight years of banking and accounting experience and my recently minted CPA credential, I decided it would be best if someone in the vetting business represented me, to help distinguish little Greg Smith among other candidates. I interviewed with several placement agencies, and eventually—per a friend's recommendation—landed in the office of Chuck Nelson.

Chuck was ten years my senior and worked for a one-off executive search agency. I was immediately intrigued by him. Unlike the other agents of the national search firms I was considering, Chuck asked me pointed questions that challenged my thinking and helped me truly consider what I wanted to do with this next significant step in my career. Even though Chuck worked on a commission basis—meaning he lived transaction to transaction—it felt like he genuinely wanted to build a relationship with me, to know me, to find the right fit for me. This was an easy decision: I knew Chuck was my guy.

Over several months, Chuck and I had some deep discussions about how I would feel in particular situations. I explained to him that I liked diversity, challenges, and solving tricky business problems. Most importantly, I was itching to be on the front lines where there was excitement, high stakes, accountability, and financial reward for a job well done. I wanted to work with or for someone who had been successful in business, someone who I could learn from, someone who could inspire me and push me to grow.

Chuck was an unexpected mentor and advisor on my path. He was someone I could talk to and be honest with, someone that listened and asked insightful questions, and my time working with him truly helped me find my way. I think mentors come in all shapes and sizes, often unexpectedly. We have to maintain a posture of openness to all people, recognizing that these treasured guides aren't usually marketing themselves as such. Sometimes it's a conversation with a stranger that changes how you perceive a decision. Sometimes it's a longtime friend who coaches you through a difficult season. And sometimes it's a Chuck Nelson—a single-man search firm who was sincerely committed to placing me in the right position with the right person.

I had everything to gain by being completely truthful with Chuck. (And this was a true potential win-win situation—he himself was compensated based on a successful placement.) I knew I didn't want to work for a big company, where I would get lost in a crowd. I wanted to work for a smaller business, where I could make an impact, so Chuck set up interviews with numerous business owners and high-net-worth (HNW) patriarchs. These were opportunities for me to home in on my desires, on my vision of the future. Who would

I become? What kind of impact did I want to have? What was I capable of? And where did I fit?

MONKEY BUSINESS

I met Saul Goldman in Duluth, Minnesota, at his offices in an old, historic flour-milling building near Lake Superior, established in 1880, a building that Saul had bought and restored with a pile of financial incentives from the state and the Minnesota Historical Society. He had a reputation as a buy-and-flip deal maker—purchasing business conglomerates, splitting up the pieces, and devolving them into other enterprises. In his world, the bits and pieces were worth more than the whole, thus he was often referred to as Liquidator Saul in national and local publications.

Saul had a big financial appetite (hence the purchases of entire conglomerates) and also invested in surplus inventories that needed to be sold, often at discount prices through big-name stores. He moved a lot of merchandise, including, as a young man, a stock of imported monkeys from India that were sold as pets (unfortunately, most of the monkeys died, but not before Saul made money off of them).

This sounded like an interesting endeavor.

Saul was surrounded by various deputies who would do his bidding: powerful lawyers, a former banker, and others. Where would I fit in this equation? At the time, Liquidator Saul had found himself in the banking business essentially overnight, after buying a string of eighteen banks that were assembled into a publicly traded bank holding company. My job would be smack-dab in the middle of this, traveling the circuit of banks, performing internal audits, and making recommendations to improve operational efficiency. Exciting stuff!

In this initial meeting, Saul was talking about all that he wanted to do with the banks. Now Saul had never owned or run a government-regulated business, like a bank. But I knew—from working in banks, alongside bank regulators—that he could never do the things he was talking about. I could see this acquisition would take years for Saul to digest, to prove that he would stay within the boundaries of normal bank operations and not run these assets like personal piggy banks. There were too many hoops to jump through, too many unpredictable, uncontrollable factors.

While Saul was a great guy, it was clear from the very get-go that his ego was running the show, and I knew I needed a break from that style of "leadership" (if you would even call it that). Would it be fun to work for this guy? Sure. But it would be like working in the circus. And it turns out, much of the circus isn't real (I hate to break it to you, but the tall guys in the circus are on stilts).

I turned this offer down and headed to my next interview.

SHINY SUITS

I met the gatekeepers for Billy Knight on the top floor of the old, restored Hammond Medical Office Building in Minneapolis. As I stepped across the threshold, the mood felt quiet and sedate. The team explained that Knight owned an insurance agency, and while his world revolved around insurance, he would occasionally diversify and buy a small community bank (back then, it was much easier to purchase a bank than it is today). At the time, Knight owned a few banks, but it quickly became clear to me that they may as well have been lumber stores or a couple of gas stations. There didn't seem to be a lot of strategy behind owning these businesses, and these guys were not bankers.

His team clearly didn't pick up on my initial hesitation, as they told me to head on up to the top floor, where I would meet Knight. I thought I *was* on the top floor, but I kept my mouth shut. Right before my eyes, a paneled wall opened up to a grand staircase of clear plexiglass steps and a single, gold handrailing. As I began my ascent up the "glass staircase," the doors slid shut behind me, and I looked up to see clouds. *Was this the real staircase to heaven?* I wondered.

Indeed, Knight had built a penthouse on the roof, with three wind-break glass exterior walls and one more devoted to a beastly fireplace. In front of this monstrosity was a sunken-floor sitting area that he referred to as "the lounge." His desk, boardroom table, and secretarial station were on the perimeter.

Had I been transported into a James Bond movie? Was I going to be released through a trapdoor into a shark pit if I refused this position? Yes, it was all ridiculously cool, but the real me—ego aside—was sensing something very awkward and very false. The dramatic effect was a bit too much. What was this hoopla all about? How long would it last?

I recall that Knight wore the shiniest suit I had ever seen in my life, all silk. During the conversation, he mentioned that—if I were offered the job—I would travel by air from one business to the next in his private plane. He had his hand in all sorts of stuff, but the truth was that most of these companies were average performers. These were small companies, disposable and interchangeable to Knight, and because of this indifferent attitude about a focus in one industry, I just couldn't see them amounting to anything under his leadership. While I could see myself being successful in this position, and certainly enjoying a private plane and some new spiffy outfits, this opportunity simply didn't feel right.

PROJECTION

The entire interviewing process (that included fourteen corporate interviews), though time-consuming, was priceless. I got a peek into the positions and lives of wealthy business moguls and had down-to-earth conversations with some of the executives that I would potentially be working with. Some were a little *too* honest, sharing details and insights that were not altogether reassuring. These interviews helped me identify the direction I wanted to go. The comparisons enabled me to envision myself a few years into the future in several different situations and allowed me the chance to sincerely consider: what did I want my future to look like?

Chuck Nelson was starting to sound a bit perplexed. He couldn't believe I was turning down these incredible offers with prominent HNW families. Wasn't this what I wanted? What I had requested? I had a hard time finding the words to explain my gut feelings to Chuck, especially recognizing that there was nothing in this for him unless I accepted an offer. But he was outrageously patient and compassionate and seemed to understand that I wanted to make the best choice that I could, that I would know it when I could feel it.

My two years at the firm were quickly running out, and the holidays were upon us. Chuck informed me that the interviews would likely come to a standstill soon and resume in January, after the new year. I forced myself not to have second thoughts about the offers I had passed up and the other positions I had simply not pursued. In the decision-making moments, I was confident, and I didn't want to lose sight of that certainty. These jobs didn't feel right, and I didn't want to sacrifice my values or my potential when the pressure was on. I knew that if I could find the right successful entrepreneur with some sound business philosophies, I could learn quickly and make meaningful contributions at the same time.

I was committed to waiting for the right opportunity.

While we can never truly foretell the future (except for the select few who read crystal balls like roadmaps, I suppose), I do think we can envision the future and project what we think might happen with the choices that we make. We have to imagine actually living with a particular course of action: Will I be proud of this decision? Can I see myself doing this thing? Can I defend this choice, if necessary? Where might this lead? Is this going to make me happy?

I believe projection is essential for a most meaningful life, for *your* life. We are all capable of choice. But it's easy for us to let our environment, facts, circumstances, family, and friends push us in one direction or another, overwhelming our own voice and internal *knowing* with opinions and judgments. Soon, it is not our life at all but a series of whimsical events that have nothing to do with each other, and that burn our precious time here on earth.

We can't know the future, but we can identify a meaningful goal, project it in our mind, and envision multiple paths that lead to achieving that goal. Then, we can put ourselves on one of those paths to achieve it. Will the path be the right one? No one knows. Will it be the most efficient? Probably not. Will the journey be meaningful? Yes, absolutely! Every journey and experience we have is our teacher: good or bad.

When I was at this crossroads in my life—choosing between several different high-net-worth moguls—I had to envision my future. These were all incredible opportunities that would lead me in specific directions, toward a future that I could only envision, not know. Had I been desperate or lacking confidence, I would have taken the first job offered to me. But I knew there were more options, more people I had to meet. I had this sense that I needed to be patient, to wait for the *right* opportunity. Not to mention, I was dealing with someone that I thought was pretty important—me! I was worth the investment, the time, and the patience.

At that point in the process, I didn't feel confident that the present opportunities would help shape me and my picture of the future. They were each fascinating, but I had to control my interest in each to truly focus on me and my feelings. This required intense introspection, asking myself what I liked and what I didn't like, and answering honestly and completely. It soon became clear: I wanted the least risk and the biggest opportunity, and if I couldn't find it, I would stay at the CPA firm a while longer (though the time away interviewing during normal business days had become glaringly obvious).

WORTH THE WAIT

Chuck called two weeks before Christmas and said he had found what he believed would be a near perfect match. The business owner had previously risen swiftly in a large family-owned bank (but was not part of the family himself). He had left said bank and, within six years, had acquired three small community banks and established a bank holding company in Newton, a small suburban town of about four hundred people just outside of Minneapolis. He had three more banks lined up to purchase, subject to regulatory approvals, and his small corporate staff was ready for an addition to take on the influx of work.

The interview was scheduled for the following Monday, if I could swing a quick trip. Before hanging up with Chuck, it occurred to me to ask, "What did you mean by *near* perfect?"

Chuck explained that he had gone out to meet the owner himself and that this was no doubt a man who held exceedingly high expectations. "It might be hard to keep him happy," he explained.

Near perfect? I thought. *This sounds just right.* Doing quality work and solving problems inside of a growing organization where high expectations were the standard sounded like a dream. And I thought with my credentials and—more importantly—my experience analyzing all kinds of businesses and identifying ways to fix them, I might just be this guy's dream too!

A few days later, I made my way to Newton, a *really* small town just off the freeway, with one bank, one gas station, two bars, and a Subway sandwich shop. The bank building was a simple, unpretentious block building, and I easily found my way to the bank holding company offices on the second floor. The staff consisted of the owner, Mr. Levitt Palmer, his secretary (Susan), a CFO (Lee), and a Chief Credit Officer (Jeff).

First, I met with Lee, who had previously worked for a large CPA firm before acquiring his current position when Mr. Palmer had started to accumulate banks. I could tell that Lee was buried in work and was informed that the position would report directly to him, with four primary tasks: help review monthly board packets, conduct periodic inspections of the banks, complete operational performance reviews, and see to the tax work. I learned that Lee hardly ever did onsite visits and that he strived for perfection, which—as it turned out—was the Palmer standard for *everything*.

The interview went well. Lee was even-tempered, thorough, and precise. I was able to be sincere about my goals, my desire to be impactful and contribute creative ideas in order to enhance the bottom line. Lee cautioned that there was a great deal to learn, but if I was willing, he would be happy to shed the work and pave the way.

I then met Jeff and Susan and was invited into Mr. Palmer's office for a meeting with him—alone. He was impeccably dressed and his office and boardroom were beautifully appointed. He had converted the second floor of this simple block building into beautiful offices, with a museum-worthy art collection. All of this told me one important thing: whatever Mr. Palmer chose to do, he did well. And he didn't need the top floor of a prestigious building in downtown Minneapolis to make a statement.

We discussed work ethic and business standards, and he seemed keenly aware of reputation risk when dealing with bank regulators. It was clear to me that he was planning to build a fortune buying small banks in small county seat towns, a business opportunity often overlooked by other entrepreneurs. It was also clear that he held himself to the same high standards that he required of others. Strong ego? Perhaps. But there was an authenticity about his seemingly mild arrogance, something that told me he had put in the work, understood himself, and would guide me in an invaluable way. I was intrigued.

I returned to work at the CPA firm that afternoon with a strong sense of gratitude that I had been introduced to an opportunity to work for Mr. Palmer. I did some homework, asked mutual connections what they knew about this man, and discovered that Mr. Palmer had worked for a bank for ten years. This bank was owned by a very wealthy, iconic family, a family that he was not a part of. Even though he would never be able to work his way to the top in this empire, he carried himself in an almost regal, distinguished sort of way. Someone I knew told me she had happened to stick her head in the boardroom door one day (when most everyone else was out of the office) and witnessed Levitt standing on the table in stockinged feet as a tailor took his measurements for a custom suit. He was twenty-seven years old at the time. True or not? Who knows? But it suggested to me that Mr. Palmer was a driven guy, and I was impressed.

Unlike the other HNW families I had encountered, Mr. Palmer was singularly focused, something that appealed to me. Perhaps a greater risk—to not invest in multiple industries—but this focus enabled him to excel at what he was doing. And part of me wanted to emulate this success. I could feel it. I could see it. This guy exuded a superhuman self-confidence that I wanted to be around. I knew it would change me and make me a better businessman.

I felt like this was the opportunity I had been waiting for, the exact position that could propel my career forward. In between silent assurances that I was qualified for this position, I prayed that I would get a call back. When my head hit the pillow that night, I finally decided there was nothing else I could do and mindfully turned it all over to God for His help and intervention. I went to sleep, full of hope.

By 9:00 a.m. the next day, I had a call from Lee asking if I could come back for another meeting. By the end of the day, I had accepted an offer with Mr. Levitt Palmer and I was on to the next great adventure, trusting that my gut hadn't led me astray and thankful that Chuck would finally get his cut.

A KEY: PATIENCE

Question: Do you believe you're worth the time?

My parents gave me a lot of advice. But among the most important advice they imparted to me was simply to be patient. "It'll work out," they'd say. Or, "Something else is going to happen. Don't give up." Most of the time—as a young kid, with very little perspective—this guidance was just annoying and fell on deaf ears. I'd plow through things, throw fits, beat my head against a wall. But over time, I learned. And throughout my life, patience has become a mantra of sorts. Whether in relationships, decisions, my own growth, or opportunities, patience has been a strong undercurrent in everything that I've ever done.

It requires patience to think about not just short-term outcomes but to think about how a decision today will impact your life for years to come. It requires patience to listen, reason, and give deep and honest thought to choices. It requires patience to watch and wait as these decisions unfold, to trust the process. It requires patience to get to know a person, to help them realize their capabilities, and to uncover what they have to offer you. It requires patience to sit in the middle of a mess and trust that there is some good, some lesson, some hope to be found.

It certainly requires patience to make mistakes and truly learn from them.

When I was making a choice about the next step in my career path at this time, I knew that this decision was crucial. I had invested the past two years carefully positioning myself and assembling my credentials to pave a way toward a better future, both personally and professionally. I also knew the clock was ticking, that I was going to have to make a decision soon, before the opportunities themselves expired.

Patience and action: it's a balancing act. Like chess, you have to make immediate, strategic moves while still considering how each decision affects the long game. The idea of projection is helpful here—envisioning how a particular decision can open doors (or close them), considering how you will feel about a choice several years down the road. I had spent the previous two years surviving by projection, believing I would get through it all and come out the other side with multiple better opportunities. But which one would be the best one for me?

I identified many opportunities that would have been better than staying at that CPA firm, opportunities that would lead to interesting careers. It would have been easy to just pick one, stop wasting time in the interviews, and get cracking with a new employer. But I honestly cared too much about myself to jump the gun.

Many people don't wait (or can't wait) for the right opportunity. Many people seek advice or affirmation from untrustworthy sources. This is precisely the pickle that leads to mile-long résumés, new jobs with new employers every few years. We must learn to wait for the right opportunity but also not miss the boat altogether. Don't hold out (or keep changing things up) in your quest for perfection. The perfect job doesn't exist, and you likely have what it takes to be successful in many careers, across a spectrum of vocations.

If my two daughters were sitting here, they would remind me that I left out one of my favorite sayings. That is, "Time waits for no one." Eventually, we all run out of time. So don't waste it. Use your time well and make the best possible decisions you can with the information you have. When it feels right, go for it. Then own it.

Chapter 6

CAN YOU SPELL PRESIDENT?

AFTER I RECEIVED THE OFFICIAL OFFER from Palmer's office, Chuck Nelson told me, "It might be very interesting to work for Levitt Palmer. It certainly won't be easy—he's a difficult man."

I said, "What does *difficult* mean exactly?"

Then he proceeded to tell me *the rest* of the story about landing me an interview with Mr. Palmer.

When Chuck first learned that Levitt was looking for someone to help with the workload, someone with business and financial acumen and accounting credentials, he immediately thought I might be a good fit for the job. Knowing Levitt's reputation as a very private person, Chuck decided to hand-deliver my résumé to Levitt's staff and schedule a meeting with Lee, the CFO. After Lee vetted and approved my résumé, he sent Chuck straight in to meet with Mr. Palmer.

Chuck wasn't quite prepared to meet with the man himself—he figured Lee would make the decision, but Lee knew this hire would ultimately be involved in the day-to-day with Levitt, so his approval was essential. Mr. Palmer asked Chuck a handful of questions about me, and he answered them in turn. Then Levitt asked him, "Why should I pay *you* a percentage of what I'm paying him?"

Referring to Chuck's finder's fee, Mr. Palmer wanted to understand the logic behind this setup. "The more I pay him, the more I have to pay you," he stated. "Maybe I don't want to pay him anything. How does that work for you?"

Chuck started to sweat a little bit. He had never been interrogated about his finder's fee before, and he felt like he was being attacked. The fee methodology was the standard practice in the industry—why should it be questioned? Poor Chuck reported that he was so intimidated by Mr. Palmer and his questioning that he had to excuse himself to use the bathroom—twice—where he became physically ill and lost bowel control during the negotiation. This wasn't some public bathroom down the hall, either. This was Levitt's personal, private restroom right there in his office.

Difficult? I thought. In the end, I thought Mr. Palmer had a point—if you're offering a service and charging for said service, you should be able to defend your fee. He had to find out what Chuck was made of. Would he defend his fee or not? Did Chuck present the best candidate, or was he trying to be like a used car salesman and sell a Buick when Mr. Palmer was demanding a Cadillac? *Fair game*, I thought.

And, in the end, Chuck received a very fair finder's fee, while I learned a valuable insight: Mr. Palmer liked to negotiate.

ALL IN

My first day on the job with Levitt was just as I expected. Lee's desk was piled high with tax returns, extensions, and administrative paperwork. He proposed I take over the tax returns while he focused on the bank regulatory applications. Lee took delegation very seriously, and soon I had piles of files on my own desk. I was so engrossed in the work on that first day that I didn't even look up until it was dark outside and I was the only one left in the office. I called my wife and explained that I had lost track of time, rinsed out the coffee pot, set it for the next morning, and headed home.

At 7:00 a.m. the following day, I was the first to arrive. I turned on the lights and the coffeepot and got to work. Lee stopped by later to check in and asked when I had left the night before.

"Around eight or so," I replied.

"Greg, quittin' time is a little before 6:00 p.m. I have to be home to eat dinner with my family at 6:00 p.m. on the dot," he told me.

At that time, my family consisted of a working pregnant wife, a three-year-old daughter, and two sets of nearby grandparents that couldn't get enough time with their one and only grandchild. Maybe my schedule was a bit more flexible. I shared this with my wife that night. While Lee was the first to leave each day, Mr. Palmer was there late into the evening, there was always unfinished work, and we never knew what the next day would bring.

"Do what you have to do, Greg," my wife assured me. "Go for it!"

She knew the drudgery I had suffered the previous two years and that this opportunity had grabbed my full attention. She knew I wanted to give it my all.

HITTING THE ROAD

You can learn a lot about a business—especially a bank—when you pore over their financial statements and tax returns. I had five years of analyst experience, and I was eager to put my knowledge and insights to the test. I told Lee I was interested in going into the banks a few days each week to meet with the management teams and possibly offer some suggestions to improve their operations.

Lee discussed this with Mr. Palmer, who thought it sounded like a great idea. He coached me on the backgrounds of various bank presidents and his own hunches about where they could improve operations. Then he had his secretary fire off a memo to each of the bank presidents, notifying them that I would be visiting all of the banks on a rotation to do an "operational review," and I rearranged my schedule to be on the road two days a week.

One of my first bank visits was in a blue-collar suburb of Minneapolis. The president, Mr. Arthur (Art) Olson, and his former shareholders, who were local businessmen, had recently sold their bank to Mr. Palmer. Art remained in charge and had adapted to most of the new loan underwriting parameters of our organization. When I showed up, he introduced me to the officers and some of the staff and began to share openly and honestly with me. I listened. Carefully.

And I heard many interesting details. Though this was a small standalone bank, Art had built an infrastructure capable of supporting a bank ten times larger. In other words, he had way too many employees! Most of these folks were stretching their work to fill an eight-hour day—it was make-work, and everybody knew it. Why hadn't someone said something? They had gotten by without raising their hands and Art was just fine with that. No disruptions. No problems. And, besides, the customers *loved* these people.

Good ole Art was in his second term as president. Prior to taking this throne, he had launched his professional life as a meat butcher, gradually working his way up the ladder to become the sole owner of a grocery store. At some point, he and some other community members had decided the town needed a bank. So Art moved the grocery store to another location, sold that business, and converted the grocery store building into a bank. He built a long, old-fashioned teller line and a bunch of drive-up lanes and proceeded to hire a whole lot of people too. Turns out grocery store cashiers made pretty good bank tellers!

These bank employees were friends of Art's—many beyond their retirement years—and Art carried them with compassion. These folks were relentlessly kind (no wonder Art wanted to keep them around!). One woman explained that, after Art had sold the bank and the new owner (i.e., Mr. Palmer) started raising overdraft fees, she spent her days calling customers who were nearing an overdraft to encourage them to come in so she could record a deposit and mitigate the fees. If they weren't able to pay it, she would simply waive the fee. As I looked into it, it just so happened that the bank had waived quite a number of different kinds of fees!

After a week's evaluation, I drafted a report and a new staffing model that proposed the elimination of twelve positions (25 percent of the staff), along with a plan to absorb work within the remaining infrastructure. This would still allow for plenty of growth, if it ever were to occur. I determined the total waived fees and suggested an overhaul of fees and interest rates. I also set up a control over these changes so that deviations would pop out on a windshield report.

I was proud of this report. It exhibited my five years of analytical work paired with what I had learned as a CPA. The report pulled the cover back on long-ignored practices and provided meaningful actionable information. Finally—I had landed the right job in the right place at the right time. I could add real value.

MR. PRESIDENT

I decided to hand-deliver the report to Art. I wanted to be straightforward and candid with him and suspected he would not welcome this intervention on "his" bank. When I walked into his office, he was dozing off after a late lunch. I told him that it was my last day in his bank (he smiled). I then handed him my report (he frowned) and explained that we should talk through it before I sent it to Mr. Palmer. Art was now awake.

He read through the report and I could see him moving faster and faster through the pages, skipping over entire sections and growing more red in the face as he went. He was clearly no longer the friendly old fellow I had first met. I was just hoping he didn't have a butcher's meat cleaver in his desk drawer.

After he finished, he stood up and threw the report on his desk.

"There is nothing to talk about," he said. "Can you spell president, Greg?"

I decided not to respond.

"If not, you can read it right here," he said, pointing to the bronze desk plaque in front of me. "As the president, I am fully empowered by the board of directors to run this bank however I see fit."

Art sat back down behind his presidential plaque and said, "No punk thirty-year-old kid is going to tell me anything about running a business. It's best you leave and take this f**king report with you."

Good ole Art had left the building. In his place, Mr. President had arrived in all of his egotistical glory. I figured this was likely not a great time to engage Art rationally, so I simply told him I was available when and if he wanted to discuss the report.

"If I don't hear from you soon, Art," I said, "I'll have to give the report to Mr. Palmer. I understand that the board empowers the president, but the board is also elected by the shareholders. And Mr. Palmer is the sole shareholder."

That got me a slammed door on my way out, but I knew it needed to be said. The bank had changed ownership and the sellers were paid well for it, including Art. But now he was accountable to a new shareholder, and Mr. Palmer wouldn't stand for a needless staffing burden. Things were going to have to change.

I had made a serious bet that Mr. Palmer would back my recommendation. While I considered the hundreds of ways it could play out, I ultimately took the long view that, one way or another, Mr. Palmer would not want to leave earnings on the table year over year. Plus, this could also send a signal to all the presidents that Mr. Palmer (or me, as it turned out) would be inspecting what he expected. And he always set the bar high for performance—even for himself!

LOVE AND LOGIC

After a week of radio silence from Art (and several unreturned phone calls), I gave Mr. Palmer the report and elaborated on my exit review with Art. Levitt smiled when I told him about Art calling me a "punk kid." He said, "Let that go. We have a lot of Arts in the organization and it's past time to shake things up. Greg, hire someone to do all of the tax and government reporting work under your direction, and you get out there and spend more time in the banks."

As I was leaving his office, he added, "And call Jack. Give him your flight schedule a week in advance."

"Flight schedule?" I said. "I'm pleased to drive my company car."

He looked up and shook his head. "Call Jack and get busy."

Mr. Palmer owned a private aircraft and he had just made it available to me. Not only did this mean that I could get exponentially more done in a day (not having to spend hours driving from place to place), but it also communicated to all the bankers that the work I was doing was important enough to warrant a plane and crew at my disposal.

A few days later, Mr. Palmer's assistant, Susan, asked me to block off time for lunch in Mr. Palmer's boardroom on Friday at noon sharp. "Don't be late," she said.

When I entered the room, I was stunned. China, crystal, and a silk-embroidered tablecloth had transformed the Kittinger boardroom table into an elegant setting for three. I went to find Susan in our small executive kitchen, where she was pulling lunch out of the oven.

"Who's the third guest?" I asked, assuming it surely must be someone exciting for all of this grandeur.

"You'll find out soon enough," she said, with a wink.

When I walked back into the boardroom, Art was seated at the table. I stared at him and he stared back at me, more stunned than I was. I crossed my fingers and hoped this wouldn't turn into a food fight. When Mr. Palmer arrived, Susan poured the wine and served the lunch, and Levitt regaled us with stories of recent hunting trips, current bank regulatory happenings, and the world economy. Art was fully engaged and enjoying every minute of it.

Eventually, Mr. Palmer turned to Art and said, "About this report…" right as Susan entered the room with three bound copies of my findings. "Greg here concludes that your staff has waived off a large sum of money in the form of fees, points, and discounted loan rates over many years. And that the operation of the bank would run well with twelve fewer employees, while still accommodating growth."

Mr. President was clearly crushed but did his best to defend himself: these were loyal employees; the customers loved these people; letting them go would affect the bank's reputation. "I can make some of the recommended changes," he concluded. "But as for the staffing, I'll have to think about it."

Mr. Palmer smiled and told Art to go ahead and think about it. "But by next Friday, I need you to write a report stating that twelve people are gone, or I'll make the list myself."

Mr. President had just received a command order from the sole shareholder and now understood that his title did not empower him as much as he thought. Although Mr. President had a choice, I knew he would make the right one and for the right reasons. He loved his position, the bank, and the employees. I suspected he'd known all along that with the change in control (the sale), staffing reductions were inevitable. I think he also wanted to see how far he could push me and his agenda. Not far.

The following Friday, Art sent me and Levitt a report identifying changes to bank fees, points, and interest rates, as well as a list of twelve names and exit dates. Mr. Palmer asked me to respond on his behalf, noting that all of Art's plans were acceptable and that I would return to his bank in thirty days to ensure that all of the changes had been made.

When I met with Art again a month later, he was civil and professional, invigorated by the modifications he had implemented. He even asked me to join him for lunch at his country club, where he apologized for his behavior and invited me to share additional pearls of wisdom to improve the financial performance of the bank. I think, in the end, Art wanted to be the bigger man, and he knew he'd be way better off with my help and the ideas I could bring to him from the other banks.

Within a year, Art's bank was among the top-performing banks in the state (as were almost all of Mr. Palmer's banks). During later years at bank presidential outings, good ole Art always engaged me in friendly conversations and genuinely respected Mr. Palmer and myself. He and his wife, Helen, though thirty years older than us, became dear friends of mine and my wife's.

EMPOWERMENT

Many of the tasks I encountered in the coming months were entirely new to me. If there was ever a question about what I should do, Levitt's response was always in the third person. I'd tell him, "We've got a few alternatives here. I've given a lot of thought to each one. I want to find out how you think we should handle this."

He would say, "Well, shouldn't you know how I would handle this? Do what Levitt Palmer would do" (as if he wasn't sitting directly across from me).

Needless to say, he didn't make it easy. And at times he reminded me of my French professor in college. He would never come right out and tell me what to do. Whether it was meeting with a bunch of bank regulators in Washington, DC, initiating a meeting with a state banking commissioner in Colorado, or (later) operating an airline, Levitt empowered me to fix problems and achieve his expectations, which of course had to become *my* expectations and the expectations I then had to communicate and instill in others.

At the same time, he allowed me to take risks, to find out what was going to work and what wasn't. I learned to think about decisions in a broader way. While the task was to achieve the best outcomes for Mr. Palmer, I took the liberty to broaden my considerations to determine who would be affected by this choice and how: Which employees? Which companies? Which vendors? What is the impact now? How about three years from now?

I made plenty of mistakes along the way. But I learned how to make decisions incrementally to manage risk. And I learned to work *with* people. A lot of people. You see, Mr. Palmer ended up owning a lot of banks in many geographic regions. There was no way I could run one of these banks, let alone three or five or dozens! There were people out there who held these positions, and each one of these individuals was only entitled to a job so long as they did said job and met the expectations of the sole shareholder, Mr. Palmer. Levitt expected every bank president to set a standard of excellence that matched his own. But he was remote, sometimes off the grid, possibly on a private 180-foot Holland midship across the globe. So I was the face of the Levitt Palmer family, the enforcer of sorts, the surrogate for the shareholder, Levitt's representative. And I was sometimes asked, "Who the hell are you?"

Levitt's reputation preceded him everywhere I went, and his reputation was *earned*. Mr. Palmer had achieved great financial success by holding himself accountable to this exceedingly high standard.

He had done the work and had accumulated tremendous financial wealth. This was an unparalleled opportunity to understand how all of these businesses worked—mergers and acquisitions and many, many business practices.

What I learned in these twenty years was absolutely invaluable. I could have worked for free and had the better end of the bargain, just for what I learned from Mr. Palmer and my experiences there. And the work itself was exhilarating—managing multi-hundred-millions of dollars—I was the least bored person in the world! To think that my two years of drudgery, my two years enduring Alan's bullying, would lead here. It was worth the wait. It was worth more than the wait.

A KEY: CHOICE

Question: Do you own your decisions?

Choice is empowering, whether you're a toddler picking out shoes to wear or a grown man deciding how to run your business. If a person gets to *choose*, they're far more likely to own their choice, the inherent risks, and even the failures (if it comes to that). When the ball is put in their court, most people take the decision-making process seriously and consider how the choice will affect others.

Levitt gave Art a choice: make a decision on which employees to cut at the bank or I'll make it for you. He never stripped Art of his power or forced his hand. He gave him two choices that would provide the results that Levitt desired, allowing Art the opportunity to save face and do his job as the president.

This was an invaluable lesson for me. I was a young punk kid compared to the presidents running the banks. And while Levitt had authorized me to implement changes, I had to be damn careful with this authority—that I didn't let it feed my ego and that I achieved results without tipping over the apple cart in each bank. I couldn't afford to burn bridges and I needed folks to buy in. I wasn't going to get far with demands and ultimatums.

So I took a play from Mr. Palmer's playbook and began compiling a list of improvements, straight from the mouths of the bank employees themselves (all of which I knew would lead to the results we wanted). Betty, the cashier in Madison, Wisconsin, said we should do this. Lonnie, the lender in Worthington, Minnesota, suggested this brilliant idea. I'd encourage other banks to contact these people directly, to talk through how they implemented the change and the ensuing results. Pretty soon, the banks were feeding off of each other's best practices and it was all of their ideas in the first place. They got to choose what changes to make, and all of these changes led to better-run banks. Talk about buy-in! Talk about a win-win.

In the end, because of this exchange of information and empowerment, every single one of Mr. Palmer's banks were among the top ten performing banks in their respective states.

It's difficult to compel someone to do something simply because you want them to or think they should. Particularly if you haven't built trust or earned the right to be heard. We don't always have the luxury of time to establish these strong foundations in a professional setting, so we have to get creative about how to get people on board, to show them (not tell them) that certain changes might be in their best interest. And the quickest way to do this is to let them decide for themselves.

If you want someone to do something, give them the chance to choose. Listen long enough to understand where the resistance is coming from, ask about possible solutions that *they* see, and then allow them to come to their own conclusions. Then, empower them to take control and bring others along with them. The act of choosing is defining because the chooser gets to own the choice *and* the consequences. If it all works out, great—they take the credit. If it fails, they own it and learn a valuable lesson (and make the next choice to fix it). You may not be able to grant choice in every situation, due to importance, risk, and complexity. But you can almost always encourage a collaboration, where your associates have a chance to express their ideas, build consensus, and act on a plan.

Chapter 7

CHANGING PERCEPTIONS

IN 1992, LEVITT ACQUIRED a bank in Helena, Montana, and prior to our final closing date, I was dispatched to inspect the business and meet with Mr. Mitch Reynolds, the bank president. I flew to Montana in Levitt's private plane, rented a car, and made my way to The First National Bank of Lewis and Clark County—the oldest bank in the county with a charter over one hundred years old—a two-story, square-box, white-brick building.

Sporting a spiffy suit and tie, leather briefcase in tow, I walked in and told the teller, "I'm here to see Mitch Reynolds."

"He's not here," she replied.

"Oh, well, I have an appointment with him at ten o'clock," I replied.

"Well, you walked right past him," she said.

"I thought you said he's not here?"

"No, he's not here. He's outside."

So I made my way back outside, where there was a ladder leaning against the building. At the top of this ladder, two stories up, was a man hanging a string of colorful Christmas lights.

I hollered up, "Are you Mitch Reynolds?"

He said, "Yeah! What do you want?"

I said, "I have an appointment with you at ten o'clock. I'm Greg Smith from Minneapolis!"

He said, "I'll be right down! Do you mind holding that ladder for me?"

Mitch Reynolds finished stringing the lights and soon stood before me on the sidewalk, tool belt strapped around his waist, Carhartt jacket hanging open, and a baseball cap over a long, white ponytail that stopped at his midback.

I said, "It's a real pleasure to meet you, Mr. Reynolds. I'm looking forward to getting to know you and learning a bit about the bank here. I represent the Levitt Palmer family, the people who your bank owners are selling the bank to."

"That's fine," he said. "But if you think you're going to make any progress with my bank in this town, you need to understand something."

"What's that?" I asked.

Without saying another word, he reached toward my neck, grabbed my neck tie, and in one fell swoop, pulled a twelve-inch Bowie knife out of his tool belt and hacked off my tie. The whole time, I was thinking he was going to cut my head off, too, so I was nothing but relieved when that knife made its way back to the belt and my necktie was the only thing dangling from his hand.

"You get the picture?" he said, as he shoved my tie into his toolbelt as well.

I said, "Mitch, I think I've got the picture," as I carefully untied what was left of my tie and unbuttoned a few buttons on my dress shirt.

This was a lesson in small-mountain-town bank culture. And I should have seen it coming! Mitch had every right to be agitated, considering his bank was about to change hands again. And considering that I had forgotten a crucial step in the process: I hadn't put myself in his shoes. I hadn't taken the time to imagine how disruptive my visit and the subsequent changes would be for him and his employees. Mitch actually did me a favor by putting me in my place and demonstrating that he didn't just hold the title of Bank President; he was one of the most revered guys in the community and therefore an essential piece of the puzzle moving forward if we outsiders were to be successful in Lewis and Clark County. Next time, I'd be sure to throw on a ski sweater and cowboy boots to show my respect.

EGO ASIDE

Now, I could have gone into our meeting that day with my ego ignited, ready to put Mitch Reynolds in his place. After all, this sale was going to happen whether he liked it or not (and whether he liked my choice of attire or not too). And at the end of the day, Mr. Reynolds was going to have to answer to Mr. Palmer or find himself a new job. But to me, that's not the way to navigate these conversations. We were ultimately talking about change, and change is difficult for people because it suggests someone is about to give up control. No one enjoys not having control. I thought, likely, Mitch Reynolds was feeling pushed around a bit.

So that day, I asked questions. A lot of them. And I listened. Because I truly believe that most people just want to be heard, to feel seen, to be invited into the process. Asking the right questions is often far more important than knowing the right answer. And listening is even more important than asking questions. You'll always learn more by listening than talking.

Mitch and I became fast friends, but—as I had guessed—he didn't want the bank to be sold. He didn't want to learn the nuances of a new shareholder, and he was happy with things as they were. I learned a lot from Mr. Reynolds that day: about his town, the surrounding areas, the potential business opportunities, and his wife, who was a successful Realtor in the area.

Mitch was a human being, with employees and a family and a passionate investment in this business, in a town that he loved and knew far better than I ever would. I wasn't the expert in this situation—he was. And he was in the midst of a change that he had no say in. My job was to listen, to try to understand, and to help guide him into seeing opportunities where he was only able to see inconveniences. This change of regime had the potential to benefit him tremendously, but me coming in, donning a fancy suit and leather briefcase, rattling off all the reasons why he should be pleased would not have gotten me far (actually, I really may have lost my head that day).

We got to talking about the possibilities that opened up with this change of hands, and he started to see a bigger picture: maybe they could open a couple of other branches in different places, put more capital into the bank, hire some more people. He thought that this sounded like a pretty good idea. And in fact, it was *his* idea. By the end of this conversation, Mitch was on board.

It's always easier to get someone to do something or believe something because they are convinced that it was their idea and the best way to proceed. If the goal is mutual alignment, it shouldn't matter who takes the credit. You get to move forward with willing partners who will lead their troops because they have *chosen* to believe. It was their choice.

I should have been more prepared to meet Mitch where he was at, as I had already seen this dozens of times in other small towns where I represented the Palmer family in their acquisitions of county-seat banks. We kept the presidents and their top management in place. We left the name of the bank the same and even encouraged the board of directors to stay on and join us moving forward, with the least disruption possible.

Over time, I introduced best practices from other banks to the newly acquired bank and let the president evaluate for himself the merit in change. This involved speaking with other presidents in the system, who were almost always advocates given their experiences, results, and successes with the changes we introduced.

Helena, Montana, was no exception and we didn't have to force anything. In just a few years, Mitch was opening up new branches throughout the state with tremendous success because the bank had the financial resources to do it. And Mitch was a *willing partner*, willing to provide the local leadership required to pull it off. The First National Bank of Lewis and Clark County went on to become one of the most profitable banks in the state of Montana, expertly operated by Mr. Mitch Reynolds. Soon, a few of us were sporting ponytails too!

FACE TO FACE

Mr. Palmer wasn't the type of person to become a partner because, quite frankly, he didn't like the idea of investing his time and money for 50 percent of anything. Plus, he liked to be in control. One of his few "partners" was a man by the name of Rick Hamilton, an old college buddy, who called Levitt one afternoon to tell him about a bank in Albuquerque, New Mexico, that he thought they should buy.

Rick informed us that Jerry Martinez, the bank president, who was also a prominent shareholder, had gathered all of the shares from the other investors (there's a heck of a lot of them in Albuquerque) and was ready to hand them all over so that we could buy 100 percent control of the bank: a $250 million bank, mind you.

"Are you sure we can get full control and all the shares?" Mr. Palmer asked.

"Yes," Rick said. "I'm sure. Send Greg to Albuquerque and have him put the deal together."

So—in the spring of 1993—I made my way to Albuquerque to meet with Mr. Jerry Martinez.

Upon arriving at the bank, I was greeted by Jerry, sporting a classic Western hat, an old leather suit, cowboy boots, and a Bolo tie: in my mind, a perfect representation of the Southwest. I was wearing cowboy boots, slacks, and a sports coat. No tie this time—I wasn't taking any chances!

"I suppose you're here to buy the bank," he said, talking around a very large wad of chewing tobacco.

"I'm here to examine the bank and meet you," I replied. "We've got a few things to talk about today."

Over the course of our conversation, we discussed the process, evaluation, and price per share. We also talked about his family and his ranch, and I came to discover that Jerry was a prominent figure in the community. Everybody knew Jerry Martinez in Albuquerque!

At the end of our initial talk, he showed me to a boardroom, where he had lined up all of the shareholder certificates for my review.

He said, "I'm going to lunch. When I come back, we can sit down and talk about it. You go on and get to work."

So I did. In the piles of papers and boxes—including journals, bylaws, and meeting minutes dating back to 1890—I found a stock ledger of certificates that had been issued to all of the shareholders of the bank, local investors that included the town doctor, mortician, and owner of the neighborhood hardware store. I knew there were three million outstanding shares of the bank, but I soon discovered that only half were represented in those documents. Where were the rest of the shares?

"How's it going?" Jerry interrupted my investigation an hour later.

"There are a lot of records here," I said, "but we seem to be missing some. I've identified a million six of the three million shares. That's over 50 percent. But what about everybody else? Do you have them lined up too?"

"Well, no," said Jerry.

"Jerry, we came down here to buy the bank…the *whole* bank. From *all* of the shareholders. And we've agreed on a price. And you've only lined up 51 percent of the bank?"

He said, "That's the deal. If you want to buy the rest, go and get it."

I looked down at the stack of papers on the boardroom table. "You've lined up 14 people here that own these shares," I said. "But the rest of the shares consist of about 340 people in this community."

"Yep," he said. "That's right."

"You're telling me that I need to go out and talk to over 300 people about selling their shares?"

"Yep," he said.

"This was *your* job, Jerry."

"That's a big job," he said.

There was no way around it: I was temporarily moving to Albuquerque to meet 340 local residents to discuss their interest in selling their portion of the bank.

Upon further discussion with Jerry, I started to get a clearer understanding of the dynamics that were at play. There wasn't just one bank building; there were branches all over the state, in towns I had never heard of, some of which had populations of less than one hundred people. But Jerry was clear—we were keeping these branches open. I began to comprehend the history and legacy of these stockholders. This bank was a hundred-year-old charter, and the current shareholders were descendants of the original owners—*his grandfather helped form the bank; his mother was a teller in the bank; her uncle used to work at the bank.*

One thing was very clear: I wasn't going to just come in with a Gatling gun and say, "Well, we own 51 percent of the bank. We're taking you all out!" That was not going to get the job done. Minority shareholders in any company, whether it's General Motors or the grocery store down the street from where you live, have dissenters' rights. They have a say; they can vote no on a merger; they can demand an appraisal. It doesn't mean they will get their way, but I wanted to avoid this potential confrontation altogether. I told Jerry to have the board of directors hire an independent appraiser to establish the value of the shares, even though we had already agreed on a price.

The appraisal came in and guess what! It said we were overpaying Jerry and the shareholders for the bank. This was no surprise to me (because when you get control of a business, you pay a little more for each share than if you were just going to buy some shares, a phenomenon known as "control premium"). But it was great news for all the investors, as the minority shareholders were going to get the same price per share as the majority shareholders—a *premium* price. This would make my job of convincing the stakeholders to sell much easier.

I told Levitt and Rick, "We'll turn this into a campaign to bring all of the financial proceeds of the sale right back to the bank, in the form of new deposits."

I couldn't wait to get this promotion started. I explained to Jerry that we could not buy his bank until every shareholder, and I meant every last one, was on board to sell. We would have one closing, and all the shareholders could come into the bank to exchange their stock certificates for a check and a special offer, available only to the former shareholders.

Sometimes, you just have to get in front of people. Face to face. There's no way around it. This was one of those times. So I rented a car and started driving to all of these tiny towns. Sometimes it would take thirty to forty minutes just to get up a person's driveway at their ranch because it was a twenty-mile-long gravel road. But, over time, I met with every single person—over bitter cups of coffee and horrible-tasting apple pies and a couple of notable mint juleps—and I got to know these folks and respect them and understand where they were coming from.

After each of these meetings, I would talk to Jerry about my conversations with his various shareholders. One day, I had just returned from sharing a cup of tea and a slice of meatloaf with an eighty-year-old woman out in Truth or Consequences, New Mexico.

"Well, did she ask you what high school you went to?" Jerry asked.

"Yeah, she sure did," I said.

"Well, that means you've won her over," Jerry assured me.

Apparently, in Albuquerque, "Where did you go to high school?" is code for "I'm willing to give you a chance." It was an open door, an opportunity to prove my genuineness and sincerity. Over the following months, I cannot tell you the number of times I answered the question, "Well, what high school did you go to?"

I put thousands of miles on that little Ford rental car. In the end, not only did we buy every shareholder out, but every last one of them came and deposited their money—we're talking $30–$40 million—right back into our bank. After the deal was done, these shareholders were coming into the bank like they were still owners. A wonderful transaction!

MOMENTUM

When change is afoot, people are almost always resistant. Threats sometimes work in these moments, although I don't recommend this path. In the case of the Albuquerque bank shareholders, empathy went a long way, really seeking to understand where these people were coming from, what motivated them, and what they wanted. I was able to build some trust and the fear of change began to melt away.

This took a lot of time. It required sitting in their chairs (literally), standing in their shoes (not literally), and getting a sense of where they were at. There was a huge distance between me—a privileged white boy from Minneapolis working for a high-net-worth family—and the individuals I met with during those months. Many of these people didn't graduate from high school. They lived in towns that struggled with crime and poor school systems. Their shares in the bank were a matter of legacy and pride.

I knew that as soon as I left those meetings, the minority shareholders would call up one of the majority owners, their people, to seek their advice and input. I had spoken with these fourteen majority stakeholders about how to handle these calls. I had told them that they couldn't really tell people what to do, that I didn't want them to take that risk. But I reminded them that they had happily agreed to sell at a price that was more than the appraisal. This was what they could share—why they had made the decision to sell, why the price was fair.

Pretty quickly, word got around. "Oh, Susie is selling? She's my granddaughter!" "Oh yes, Mike will sell. He only owns a few shares, but I gave him those shares when he graduated from high school." They all knew each other and trusted each other, and once one person heard that another was selling, they wanted to know how others had come to this conclusion. It created a positive camaraderie surrounding the selling of shares. Buy-in is a way better motivator than dictation.

You can feel it—when people start coming together, when a consensus is reached. People realize there is a mutual interest in doing something different, and all of a sudden change isn't so negative. It's not a hardship. It could be fun, actually. Rewarding. Purposeful. Maybe people figure out it's in their best interest. Maybe they begin to take ownership—*ya know, it's a good thing I thought of this*. Then they have absolutely convinced themselves that they're moving forward with this change. They're not just hoping or wishing for it. They *believe* it. And they're going to bring a bunch of people along with them. This is the kind of momentum that is unstoppable, and when it works in your favor, it's exciting and fun.

When you envision a goal, make a plan, share this with others, and get those people on board as advocates, this creates momentum. If our goal is to help others see that a certain change might be in their best interests, we have to give them ample time to consider their choices, rather than forcing or blindsiding them. Once a few people come along and buy into the change, momentum happens. The change becomes contagious, almost self-fulfilling. And momentum is a powerful force. Momentum evokes big change.

A KEY: FLEXIBILITY

Question: Are you willing to put yourself in another person's shoes?

When I first arrived in Albuquerque, I had a plan in mind to handle the situation based on the facts I was given. Once I learned the facts had no foundation in truth, I had to change my plans; so much so that I had to move to and live in Albuquerque for six months! If I didn't shift course quickly, I would have had a disaster on my hands.

No different than waltzing into Helena, Montana, dressed like a finance guy from the big city, only to have the bank CEO nearly slice my throat open for my choice in attire. I had inadvertently cast the wrong impression, which was interpreted as the wrong attitude, which worked against me. I had gotten in my own way.

In these cases (and many others in my life), I had to pivot—fast. This has meant recognizing that there are real humans on the other side of the table. They have feelings, are generally averse to change, and have egos that need to be fed. Sometimes, they feel an unwavering need to win. If we dig our heels in on things that don't matter, we lose the opportunity to be successful in the really important stuff.

That means where we can give a little, we should give a little. I don't need to wear a tie and tuck in my shirt everywhere I go. That doesn't define me. What was I trying to prove? I wasn't going to get very far by demanding that Jerry hold up his end of the deal or that I would refuse to cold-call 340 shareholders in small towns throughout New Mexico. If I had chosen inflexibility in these moments, I would have lost the deals altogether and burned bridges in the process.

So much of life is about compromise—working toward the middle, finding a creative way that addresses the needs and wants of the other side without entirely sacrificing your own. Flexibility takes many forms: offering an attentive ear (being flexible with your time), considering a different perspective (being flexible with your opinions), giving an unexpected person a chance (being flexible with who you deem worthy), and the list goes on.

Not everyone is capable of change because their ego just won't let them. There are prideful human beings who will reject change just because they can and—worse—create all kinds of grief for you and others. This can lead to some powerful inertia in the wrong direction. If you see that coming, you may need to pull this person aside, before the contagion of ill will spreads. Try to uncover the real root of the problem, where the dissension originates. Finding out the why can often eliminate the opposition altogether.

For one resisting shareholder in New Mexico, I eventually (after asking and listening) discovered that her shares in the bank were one of the last tokens of remembrance she had of her grandfather, who had signed over his stock certificates to her decades before. It was highly personal. We subsequently learned that this was also the case for several others. These certificates were like a rare coin, with their silver edges, fancy print, and official seals.

How could we pay respect, honor this sentiment, and all feel satisfied? We had to take the time first to understand, to be flexible with our own desires, and then to meet them in the middle. We found a local printer who could replicate these documents. At the closing, we gave every shareholder a "deal toy" in the shape of the state of New Mexico, with an image of their certificate sealed inside. These folks loved it, and I'll bet most of them still have these monuments displayed on a shelf or a fireplace mantel, in memory of a loved one.

Chapter 8

STICK TO YOUR KNITTING

LEVITT PALMER WAS very good at identifying, investing, buying, and expanding existing bank franchises. He was singularly focused and executed a unique strategy that few bankers had discovered. This particular strategy won over the bigger lending banks who provided debt capital to enable Levitt to make ongoing acquisitions. The bank regulators also found favor with this strategy, though they had full veto power over any particular transaction (and occasionally made certain transactions difficult).

My job was to appease the bank regulators and negotiate outcomes and structures that everyone could get behind. Levitt had built his reputation on successfully closing every deal he initiated, and word got around. If we approached a prospective bank for purchase, the sellers knew ahead of time that Levitt could assemble the financing and that the bank regulators would likely approve the transaction. Talk about momentum!

This singular focus and impeccable closing rate also led to countless bank deals landing on Levitt's desk. We had lots of sellers intrigued with the idea of meeting Levitt, seeking his advice, and selling to him, if he was interested. For me, this meant appraising *a lot* of deals.

It also meant that Levitt was able to cherry-pick the ones that offered the best financial returns. But the best opportunities certainly didn't come without a list of complications. We rarely bought a bank in perfect condition—there was usually some odd set of problems that needed to be fixed, and that was also my job. The diversity and demanding nature of my responsibilities kept me on my toes. I felt inspired, challenged, and fortunate to be a part of this operation.

DIVERSIFICATION?

During my first few years working for Mr. Palmer, I was in North Carolina meeting with Rick Hamilton, when Levitt called me and told me he needed me to pick up some papers from a friend of his who happened to be a former governor of South Carolina.

I said, "Well, I'm in North Carolina, Mr. Palmer."

He said, "No, he's coming to see you at the Wilmington airport."

So I drove out to the airport to meet William "Wing" Carter, a former governor of South Carolina. I stood on the tarmac and watched as this crazy-looking airplane with an old-school propeller on the back—a Mooney aircraft or sometimes referred to as a pusher—whipped left and right in the high winds in its attempts to land safely. I thought surely I was about to witness my first plane crash. When the pilot finally got it on the ground, he opened up the hatch, long white hair and a scarf whipping behind him, threw his briefcase in the air, and bellowed out, "Vive La France!!!!!"

Was this a reincarnation of Charles Lindbergh landing in Paris after his famous flight? No. This was Wing Carter.

He jumped off the wing and opened his briefcase, and we reviewed some papers together on the top of a fifty-five-gallon oil drum in a hangar. Then, he hopped in a car and took off down the dirt road, fishtailing all the way.

Several years later, my wife and I were on a cruise and had stopped for the day on the island of St. Thomas. We were taking a stroll on the beach that afternoon when we noticed a bunch of middle-aged guys playing basketball, hooting and hollering and making quite a scene. I noticed in the bunch a tall, skinny guy with long white hair. I thought, *Well, by golly, that's Wing Carter from South Carolina!*

I went up and said hello. After some general chitchat, he informed us that he wanted to come see our cruise ship because he was thinking he would like to take a cruise someday with his wife, Heidi, and she had never been on a cruise vessel. So I called the ship and they got the captain on the line, and Wing and Heidi took a tour that same day.

As he was leaving the ship, he asked me, "How's it going with Levitt?"

"You know, it's a lot of work," I said. "A lot of challenges. Right now, Levitt is thinking about buying a chemical company that turns soybean oil into a plasticizer."

"I wouldn't do that," he said. "Greg, it's on you to be successful with the family. All those bank investments that are accumulated, you're accountable for those. If he vectors off to the left or right and gets into a chemical company, God only knows—that's on you. I think y'all should stick to your knitting."

This statement hit home with me pretty hard. The reason I had chosen to work for Mr. Palmer was his intense, singular focus on community banks. We knew them inside and out. I had no fear of learning a new industry, but measuring a new world of risk and opportunity would take time and we really had limited human resources at our bank holding company to manage other investments.

BLOWN UP

Despite my hesitations, we bought the chemical company a few weeks later. Mr. Palmer and his buddy (who brought the deal) made this decision and became partners. I don't know who they consulted with, but the deal was on. The plant was in a little midwestern prairie town where a chemical engineer (who looked more like a mad scientist) had created a supersecret formula to turn soybean oil into plasticizer. This epoxy would then get loaded into oil tanker rail cars headed to Philadelphia, Pennsylvania, where it would be transformed into a plastic wrap. Now, don't get confused—we didn't own plastic wrap. We owned the company that knew the supersecret formula, and it made a heck of a lot of money converting the molecular structure of those soybeans (whatever *that* entailed).

A PhD/chemist by the name of Dr. Howley had come up with this recipe, and this guy looked just like Doc Brown from Back to the Future—frizzy hair, white lab coat, and all. About a year after we had purchased the company, Dr. Howley called me on a Sunday morning and asked if I could come on down to the factory...right away.

I said, "I was just there last week for the board meeting, Dr. Howley. What's up?"

He said, "You know I am so sorry to intrude on your Sunday morning, but I really just need you to come."

So, a few hours later, I arrived at the factory, a four-story building surrounded by soybean fields and—this particular Sunday morning—a whole slew of fire engines. One side of the building had clearly been scorched, and the eight fire engines from neighboring towns were still just rolling up their hoses.

Dr. Howley, covered in soot, his coat torn and burned, said, "We've had a bit of an explosion here."

"I can see that," I said, "What happened?"

"Well, I never really told you guys how I make the plasticizer, what I really do to the soybean oil to cook it and turn it into epoxy," he said.

"What are you talking about?"

"Well, some people would say that we have a nuclear reactor on our hands."

I thought, *What the heck? We could have lost half the state.*

Thankfully, it was only a "small" explosion, and the machinery was still intact. But I couldn't help but think of Wing Carter's words at that moment—stick to your knitting. Maybe it would be a good idea to exit the chemical business.

EXIT PLAN

I was always honest and direct with Levitt. I had to be. And that meant telling him things that he maybe didn't want to hear. But I always told him exactly what was happening in the field because he needed to get a sense of reality, even if it was not going according to plan. And—if something happened that was not in the plan—it was my job to report it and to fix it.

So I called Levitt that Sunday morning to let him know I wouldn't be joining all the Norwegians in the Syttende Mai parade that day (where one of our Wisconsin banks had entered a parade float).

"I'm going to be researching new potential owners of the chemical company," I told him. "The problem at the plant may not be one we can fix."

At that moment, I realized how much we *didn't* know about owning a chemical company. We were in over our heads. And the possibility of dealing with insurance claims and potential regulatory action would be a humongous distraction from our commitments and obligations with multiple ongoing banking transactions.

Coincidentally, Levitt had recently received a cold call from an investment banking company in New York. The guy on the other end of the line was also a chemical engineer and knew about Mr. Palmer's chemical company acquisition. He asked Mr. Palmer if he knew what this company was worth. Of course, Mr. Palmer exclaimed that he knew *precisely* what it was worth but invited the investment banker to enlighten him. This led to several meetings and ultimately an engagement with the investment banker/engineer, who helped us sell the company.

After considerable research on prospective buyers, we narrowed the competitive selling process down to two companies: one European and one American. Eventually, the American company dropped out (but the European company didn't need to know that!). Not only did the Europeans continue bidding for the chemical company, but Levitt and his partner got a great agreement and great terms, especially considering the substantial risks being transferred to the buyer.

We made sure the buyer knew about the fire and the inherent hazards, and we disclosed every detail we knew of. This strategic buyer understood exactly what they were getting into and found it accretive to their business. Mr. Palmer was very lucky to come out of that deal with a substantial profit in a short period of time. Sometimes it's better to be lucky than smart, but Levitt was usually both.

A KEY: FOCUS

Question: What do you want to be really good at?

When I took the job with Levitt, there were plenty of people who questioned whether or not I would succeed (and whether or not I was crazy). My years with Levitt were marked by unique challenges that I had never encountered before, and this required me to constantly think creatively to find a way in, through, or around every single obstacle. It required all of my attention, nearly all of the time—a focus I was hungry for and willing to give.

I love youthful, entrepreneurial spirit: diversity, creativity, innovation. I love that young people are hustling, coming up with new ideas and looking for ways to make a difference in the world. But sometimes people try to solve problems that don't yet exist. People come up with an idea or an invention that doesn't meet a real need—a product add-on, a service, an update that no one is yet asking for. And sometimes people spread themselves so thin in the attempt to meet every need, everywhere.

When my dear friend Kasim (more on him in Chapter 13) first formed his company, Solutions 8, he was getting into all sorts of services: advertising, loyalty programs, digital marketing, website design, video production. I kept telling him, "Kasim, pick one thing and be the best at it. You can still be called Solutions 8, but pick one thing and do it really, really well. In time, if you stick with it, you'll become a recognized authority!" (I might have even regurgitated Wing Carter's "stick to your knitting!" proclamation.)

But, not unlike me in my early days with Levitt, Kasim had to find this out for himself. (Remember, mistakes can be our greatest teachers.) Kasim started offering all of these client products and services. It became a huge burden to provide everything that each client wanted. He was maxed out and frustrated, and it wasn't much fun anymore. When Kasim finally pivoted and decided to focus his efforts on one thing—digital marketing with Google Ads—his company took off. Given a singular focus, he built one of the most successful, recognized, and credentialed digital marketing agencies in the world (and I believe he's having a lot of fun doing it). Today, he is an internationally recognized thought leader on digital marketing.

This is the power of focus. This was what Wing Carter was alluding to all those years ago: focus on one thing and become the best at it. Don't get distracted.

For the twenty years I worked for Mr. Palmer, I never experienced him as anything but a very private, accomplished man who absolutely strived for perfection. He didn't just think or hope that he was a brilliant and refined person. He *was* that person. In some ways, he had become his ego (a phenomenon I have never encountered before or since). There was nothing he couldn't fix or accomplish. This was the threshold of performance that I was expected to live with, and as long as we were focused on banking, I was fine with that. Investments in other industries were not quite as predictable (as you'll find out in the next chapter, as well).

Mr. Palmer's almost singular focus on banks enabled him to think outside the box in a very traditional and predictable industry. Most bankers are happy with compounding interest every night because it's almost a sure bet. Not Levitt Palmer. Instead, he would ask, *What else is possible? What else can we do? How can we maximize the human resources and physical buildings and customer interactions?* Then I was empowered to execute his ideas. This focus and determination is precisely what allowed Levitt's company to soar to such tremendous heights.

Chapter 9

SKY'S THE LIMIT

AS I MENTIONED IN THE INTRODUCTION, Levitt Palmer decided to buy an airline company, largely motivated by potential financial gains. Despite the apparent risks, we saw plenty of accumulated cash on the balance sheet, and Mr. Palmer was not short on the financing front. The business model was all charter aviation (as opposed to scheduled air), and the planes were sold by the hour to wholesalers whose customers purchased vacation packages. If everything worked out as planned, we would pay off the acquisition debt in two or three years. After that, it would be a cash cow.

Within a year of purchasing Vacation Air, I had become the stand-in co-president and vice chairman of the board. No one wanted me there, which was glaringly obvious when the co-founder pointed me to the mop closet with a floor drain for my office. If you're ever fuming mad (I may have overreacted), I have to say that throwing bags into the belly of a plane is a great way to work off some steam. I imagine it's similar to throwing plates, except it's a little more productive, it's a much better workout, and your family will thank you for not destroying your finest dishware.

I spent a lot of that first day loading luggage, talking with employees on the tarmac, and sweating up a storm. When my arms started to give out, I went to the airline's commercial commissary kitchen to wash dishes and help make food for the flights. By lunchtime, people were wondering, *Who is this goofy looking red-headed-stepchild-of-somebody running around here?* But I had a badge, so they couldn't kick me out. After the kitchen was cleaned, I went out to the terminal and greeted all the crews coming off flights, and I didn't leave the gate until I talked to every one of our employees exiting the planes.

I wasn't fooling myself. I knew nothing about the airline business, and I wasn't about to pretend I did. There were seven hundred people involved in this operation, their CEO and other co-founder had died unexpectedly soon after the acquisition, and they all had questions, concerns, and fears.

The officers and employees all knew each other and had all come from the airline industry. Though I was the outsider, I represented the majority owner. Their friend/business partner/leader was gone and there was no way I could replace him. The other partner was equally respected, but his background was more operational. He was excellent at it, but translating operational matters into financial terms that Mr. Palmer would understand and support became my job.

There was no doubt in my mind: in adversity lies opportunity. I just had to look for it. I had to be patient. And approach this from the ground up. Since I was coming in from ground level, notwithstanding the executive title and empowerment, I got an organizational chart so I could identify the key people in each department. Then I sought each one out for a confidential chat. And I listened, with compassion, sincerity, and honesty. I heard each one of their stories.

FIRING AND HIRING

A few years after I had started to build some credibility at the airline, we had added a few planes and were on track servicing the acquisition debt, but the economy had taken a sudden volatile swing south. Discretionary spending slowed and leisure travel took the back burner. I gathered twenty-one managers around a boardroom table on a Monday morning to tell them that this airline was not going to survive unless we did something radical.

"We need to have a workforce reduction," I told them. "We need to make some furloughs and hopefully, eventually, we can hire them all back."

This was an excruciating decision. These employees had done nothing wrong and didn't see these layoffs coming. But there was no other way—we had to save the company, and the only way to do this was to rapidly reduce overhead. Since the planes were leased, missing a payment would trigger a default, so we contacted the lessors and negotiated reduced payments or skipped payments. We made other reductions in other expense categories as well, but since the planes were on the ground more than in the air, I had to address staffing levels, and everyone knew it.

Mr. Palmer was hesitant to start funding losses, so survival meant we had to reign in expenses until the charter business resumed and passengers would start flying again to their favorite leisure destinations.

I said, "Seven of you have to go by the end of the week. You choose, or I'll choose. We can afford to go forward with fourteen managers, and that team will make staffing reductions throughout the company in their various departments. And I'll take my salary to zero—I'll work for nothing. Anybody want to join me for nothing?"

Sometimes, you have to put your money where your mouth is. And, I had seen this play out successfully with good ole Art. On Friday, five days later, fourteen managers walked into the meeting. They had figured it out.

COMMON GROUND

One of the other problems muddling the waters with Vacation Air was their volatile relationship with a large scheduled carrier across the tarmac, who were outraged that Vacation Air was experimenting with scheduled airline services. Vacation Air was supposed to be a charter airline service sold through trip consolidators for leisure travel, but someone in the group had started positioning planes to do scheduled air services to St. Louis and Minneapolis, territory that the scheduled airline felt they unofficially "owned." Not only were we infringing on their territory, but we were offering flights at a fraction of their cost. Legal? Sure. Respectful? Not really.

But they couldn't flat-out tell us not to compete. *That* would be illegal. However, we were also absolutely dependent on the scheduled airline. Our pilots were trained in their flight simulators. They owned our maintenance schedule, all of our tracking software, the parts we used to fix our planes, and the company that distributed our charter business. They even owned our hangar, which we leased from them. This was not a bridge we wanted to burn. We needed them.

I figured this solution was rather simple: I needed these guys to tell me how to keep the peace, how to make them happy so we wouldn't lose everything. So I walked across the tarmac and sat down at their boardroom table with the management team. Once they got their big egos out of the way and I asked them what they wanted, I listened. And then I told them what we wanted too. I discovered that we could both have what we wanted, and the solution might actually be the key to Vacation Air rising out of the red.

They wanted Vacation Air to stick to its knitting, to quit offering scheduled flights to St. Louis. And we needed to establish a sustainable, lucrative operation. It was at that moment that I realized we needed to expand our charter flight operation by partnering with other wholesale tour operators to provide the consistent diversified business essential to staying in business.

This conversation with the big guys across the tarmac was exactly the kick in the pants we needed, and we got on the phone right away. Soon, we had multiple tour companies in multiple cities selling packaged tours and competing for access to our planes. All of a sudden, we were doing charters for all kinds of companies and had built a year-round business.

So we expanded our fleet. Over time, we grew profits to record levels. And yes, we hired back everyone who wanted to return to the airline and were able to give twenty cents of every dollar back to the employees for their profit sharing, their 401(k)s, or other retirement accounts. The unions came on the scene several times during these years, but the employees were loyal and liked the idea of profit sharing. And the airline flourished.

Years later, when the airline was sold, the new buyers replaced all our old planes with new planes, started competing for scheduled air services, and ultimately ran the airline into the ground, declaring bankruptcy. These same amazing employees would be without paychecks for over six months. The money these families had been able to put away from their profit sharing and hard work sure came in handy then. You never know how the story will unfold!

A KEY: LISTENING

Question: Will you stop talking to listen and learn?

Everyone thought I was crazy for walking across that tarmac and sitting down with the big airline folks. After all, I was willingly consorting with the enemy. They likely thought I was going to lose my head (little did they know I had already faced this fear when Mitch Reynolds went for my neck (tie). But something in me told me that if I was just willing to listen, we could find common ground. Someone in that room was likely to be reasonable, to be honest, and to be a part of finding a solution.

I figured those guys had things they wanted to tell me but that it wasn't black-and-white. There were concerns they literally couldn't voice—legally and ethically—but that didn't make these issues invalid or untrue. I had to read between the lines. I had to listen.

We all have these things on either side of our heads that are hooked up to our brains (they are called ears, for those of you that aren't tracking), but for many people, they are the least-often-used body part. I'm not kidding—most of us are downright terrible listeners! We love to hear ourselves talk, to voice our opinions and judgments and stories. But if we're always talking, we close our brains off to learning, to deeper understanding, to finding solid, mutual ground with people around us. Listening is intricately connected with learning.

In his book *How to Win Friends and Influence People,* Dale Carnegie says, "Listen first. Give your opponents a chance to talk. Let them finish. Do not resist, defend, or debate. This only raises barriers. Try to build bridges of understanding."

If we were to pause (meaning, really *stop* talking), we might discover that our stickiest problems or competitors (or even enemies!) are simply compromises and connections waiting to happen. We have to be willing to ask: *What do you need? What do you want? What are your expectations? Why are we having this disagreement? What do we need to do to move forward?* And then listen attentively to the other person's answer.

(And a word to the wise: don't fool yourself. You can't fake genuine listening. When you're not listening with genuineness, people know. They know you are blowing them off. They know when you are not actively engaged and invested in a productive dialogue. True listening requires sincerity.)

Listening is the secret to building meaningful relationships. And I'm not just talking about your spouse or your children or your closest friends (though you should absolutely practice listening in all of these relationships). Meaningful, professional relationships will make your life richer, more productive, and more enjoyable. If you can listen long enough to uncover the reason you experience conflict with a coworker, you might just find that your work life improves dramatically. If you prove to your supervisors that you are a person that pays attention to their words, seeks to understand, and carries out what they ask, you might just find yourself promoted much quicker than you anticipated. And these valuable, positive connections can go a long way in building a career, paving a path to success and happiness.

Trust is not built overnight. It has to be earned. Which often requires time and patience. I'll let you in on a secret, though: genuine, good listening expedites the trust-building process. A good listener instills confidence in the speaker. The speaker then begins to trust the listener more and more. Over time, this person will share more sensitive, honest, insightful information. Try it sometime with a total stranger (or someone you know)—ask one question the other person will find interesting and then get out of the way. Let them answer. If there is a lull in conversation, resist the urge to fill the gap. Just let them go on. Not only will you start to build a friendship based on trust, but you'll also learn a lot in the process.

Chapter 10

WHEN TO QUIT

DESPITE THE NONEXISTENCE of computers at the time, I still think I got thirty years of work done in the twenty years I worked for Mr. Palmer, thanks to an oversized cell phone, dial-up fax machines, and good ole snail mail. I worked as hard and as smart as I could, hired lots of bright people along the way, and delegated as much as I could. The authority and responsibility I was given enabled me to learn a great deal about people and relationships and about success and fear. I discovered that, at the end of the day, a person's character is everything.

In the end, we sold his entire banking organization, an incredible transaction that included over one hundred banking locations throughout the Midwest and Southwest. At that time, I didn't know if Mr. Palmer would shift to wealth preservation mode or continue empire building. All I knew was that it was a great run for me, I had learned a lot, and I had worked myself out of a job.

I thought it was time for me to form my own business, BANCO Advisors. But a couple of partners from a local CPA firm—the firm engaged to perform routine audits for many of Levitt's banks—approached me and asked if I would consider coming on board to oversee their mergers, acquisitions, and investment banking activities.

Now if you recall, this wasn't the first CPA firm I had worked for (and the first one wasn't the greatest experience of my life). But this firm wasn't looking for another CPA. They needed someone with securities credentials. I also had twenty years of experience not only buying and selling businesses but *managing* businesses (which is rare among investment bankers). It looked like a good fit. So, despite my hesitations about reentering the CPA world, I delayed forming my own business, wrote a check for $100,000, and became an equity partner in this CPA firm.

On my first day, they showed me my office—a beautiful corner space with big diagonal walls—the former office of Robert Tisdale (the founder of the firm), who was then mostly retired and had stepped aside to the smaller office right next door. This enormous office had plenty of room for a couch, a conference table, and a massive desk. But that day, it was empty.

"There's no furniture in here," I mentioned to my onboarding committee, in case they hadn't noticed.

They informed me that—in addition to writing a check for $100,000—I was also in charge of purchasing my own office furniture. "Didn't you know that?"

I sure didn't. They recommended a few furniture companies where I could purchase the standard desk, standard bookcase, and standard executive chair.

I said, "Thank you so much for that."

Having worked with bank clients in the furniture business years earlier, I knew I could purchase good quality furniture for cheap. So I called a wholesaler and described what I was looking for. I wanted to go all out! They said, "We may have exactly what you want." So I went over there and bought the whole office set for thirty cents on the dollar—the Napoleon library table, partner desk on both sides, big bookcases with curved corners, all the pullouts, and two chic side chairs. All beautiful cherry wood and brand-spankin'-new, it was delivered and installed in my corner office.

When people came into my fancy corner office, their jaws dropped. They were honestly probably wondering what I was trying to prove and who the heck I thought I was. I thought, *Well, you guys gave me Mr. Tisdale's office, for goodness' sake. And it was empty. So I had to get some furniture to fill the darn thing.* And that was the beginning of my days back inside a CPA firm.

SELLING COWS

I came into the firm to run a subsidiary that was registered to manage mergers and acquisitions, which I could do with my Series 7 securities license. My first assignment with the firm was selling a dairy company—basically a herd of livestock and dairy product manufacturing equipment—for a private family in Oregon. They were a long-time client of the firm, and the engagement was already in process when I arrived. The family was expecting around $50 million for the sale. But after reviewing the financial statements and some comparative price comps, I wondered, *What if it could sell for more? How much more?*

I started thinking outside the box about potential buyers. Maybe it wasn't a US company or a current client of our CPA firm. Maybe it wasn't someone we knew. I wanted to do some research and run a competitive process, to try to get two or three horses on the track to run the race.

I also knew that if we set the price, we were inevitably setting the ceiling. Buyers would come in and want to pay less. Instead, I wanted to let the buyers set the floor, to go up from there, particularly if we could get two or three people to bid on this asset. This was a foreign concept to the employees at the CPA firm, accountants who were accustomed to doing tax returns and audited financial statements and getting paid by the hour. But I was certain—if we were going to sell someone's company—we should try to bring about the greatest financial result for this client. And we should understand their other goals and objectives as well.

With that in mind, I arranged a premium billing for our work with the seller so that if the seller made more than the expected selling price (as I anticipated), our firm would also net more. Our interests were mutually aligned, and the seller happily agreed to the contract. It was a clear win-win.

I sold the company for $58 million to a company in Poland, a company that I had found by doing research and putting together a book to memorialize what we were selling. But the firm wouldn't let me collect the premium fee. "The bill is the bill," they said. "They're a twenty-year client of our firm, and while you've added a tremendous amount of value, we're not going to take the money. We're going to stick to the standard bill from the original agreement."

This was disheartening. Especially because the dairy farm family had already agreed to the higher payment. That's what they *expected* to pay. We were all aligned in running a competitive process to bring about the highest and best result that we possibly could for their family. That was the job, the mission, the quid pro quo. And if I hadn't put together the arrangement to help exceed their expectations, we could have just sold the company for $50 million or maybe less. I certainly didn't see the point in that—if there was more value, there was more value. For all parties involved (the additional fees were for the firm, not for me).

Turns out, there are a lot of brokers in my business who set their fees where they are not mutually aligned. This is called the reverse Lehman Formula—where they charge less on the incremental increase in the sale price. I've never thought this was a good idea. I think we should charge *more* on the increment, but these accountants definitely did not agree. They didn't want to take success fees from clients because they were accustomed to billing by the hour. They were stuck in their ways.

And this led to the same recurring concerns: *Why didn't I bill by the hour like the accountants did? Why wasn't I "accountable" for my time? How many hours did I put in on this or that?* None of these questions were relevant because my fees (that I was creating for the firm) were called success fees. They were contingency fees: if the deal got done, the firm got paid (a lot!). But it was clear that the partners didn't have their heart in this type of business. They wanted to get into the business of mergers and acquisitions, but they didn't really want to fully embrace it. At the end of the day, they expected me to operate in a way that was not consistent within the industry, and this wasn't good for either one of us.

FIRING MYSELF

I had to back up, reevaluate. This wasn't exactly what I had signed up for and certainly wasn't going to be a viable career path for me. Furthermore, the firm wouldn't find the financial success they expected by limiting financial outcomes. But, for me, this realization didn't mean duck and run. I wanted to be a part of solving a bigger issue that I recognized: perhaps they were on the wrong side of the business.

I approached the team with an idea, an idea that would ultimately eliminate my position. This involved keeping the subsidiary securities firm but changing the business side of things, eliminating capital raises, mergers, and acquisitions (the stuff I like to do). I suggested they instead shift to managing client financial portfolios, to helping their clients handle their sale proceeds in the market. If they chose to go this route, they would need to hire a registered investment advisor, and I would help them find the right person for the job.

"So we're not going to be selling these companies for hundreds of millions of dollars and taking these big fees from our clients?" they asked.

"You're not going to be selling anything," I said. "Just managing people's money, and I'll be gone. How does that sound?"

"Well, that sounds pretty good," they said.

I knew a guy by the name of Patrick "Trick" Hanson, a connection from my days working for Levitt. Trick was a stockbroker and I thought he might just be the person we were looking for. So I called him up and said, "Do you want to come and work for a securities firm owned by a CPA firm?"

And he said, "What would I do?"

I said, "Well, you're *not* going to be buying and selling any businesses, that's for sure."

It turns out that the man that ran the firm belonged to the same country club as Trick. I talked to this fella, told him I had things all lined up with Trick, if he would just take a meeting.

He said, "Oh, he belongs to my country club!"

I said, "Yeah, I know. He told me that."

So they hired Trick, and I slipped out, and we all thought this was a pretty good deal.

CONNECTIONS

What did I get out of this deal? you ask.

I got Robert Tisdale.

Robert, "semi-retired" (but, in reality, fully retired and in his mid-seventies), would occasionally shuffle into the office at nine o'clock in the morning, accountable to no one and nothing at that point in his life. At one point, this guy, as a highly revered CPA, had been the center of all activity in the city. However, by the time I arrived at his firm, Robert had effectively been kicked to the curb. He was up there in years, a little hunched over, and maybe not as spry as he once was, but I suspected this man had a wealth of wisdom and knowledge.

"Did I take your office, Mr. Tisdale?" I asked, on one of my first mornings at the firm.

"No, no, no," he said. "I only come into the office in the mornings. I put on my slippers and smoke my pipe and read the *New York Times*. I'm happy you have my old office."

I felt indebted to Mr. Tisdale for the use of his old office, and I wanted to do a really, really good job. I thought if I kept him in the loop, he might even find what I was doing interesting. While he had never dabbled in investment banking himself, he seemed to be intrigued by the idea of mergers and acquisitions, knowing that a lot of his former clients and some partners in the firm were shaping deals behind the scenes. I decided—out of respect and courtesy—that I would visit with him from time to time, bring him a cup of coffee, talk, and mostly listen. I have always believed that it's easy to be nice to people and listen. It doesn't cost us anything but a little time.

"What are you doing for lunch today?" I'd ask.

"I'm probably going to my private club down the street," he'd say. "Are you a member?"

"Nope, I'm not. But I'll go with you!"

I'd help him across the street (because the light would turn red before he could cross it), and we would enter the late 1800s ivy-colored building that had archaic designated entrances for men and women (though they didn't enforce these then). Robert was a former chairman of the club, so he would introduce me to all of the executives: from 3M, Medtronic, St. Jude's, United Health, University of Minnesota, you name it. I mean, he knew *everybody*.

I was spending time with Robert to be kind and respectful, and I also genuinely liked him. I recognized that everyone else and the world of technology had moved on, but here was a talented man that spent his life on the telephone and in face-to-face meetings with clients. He gently steered me away from certain businesses or particular people that, in his view, were dishonest or unethical. "Don't waste your time with that one," he'd say. And he would point me toward individuals and businesses who would truly see the value in what I was doing within his firm.

Robert Tisdale was another undercover mentor in my life. I didn't realize it at the time, but over numerous lunches at the club, Robert shared wisdom with me, pulled from the years of experience he had working with people in the financial world. He had a radar, of sorts, and he taught me how to discover early in a relationship whether a client would respect my knowledge and the value that I was bringing to the table.

This became an honest and true friendship. The connections he bridged for me were invaluable as I was working nearly alone at the firm, but for a few team members I had hired. These connections also gave me confidence that there was a client base that I could work with if I were to start my own business and build my own portfolio of clients. It was another step in the journey toward launching my own firm.

A KEY: HAPPINESS

Question: Are you honest and true to yourself?

After two and a half years managing the investment banking side of a CPA firm, I had become the outcast. I liked the work and I liked the partners, but there was a cultural difference that I couldn't ignore. While I was bringing revenue into the company, I was also causing grief. The accountants were conflicted about my success fees and were no longer independent to do their audit work if the client remained a client, which was almost always the case. I also knew that I didn't need to be a part of a

CPA firm to do what I wanted to do. I didn't *need* to be a fox in the chicken house. I had my own identity. I was building my own reputation.

It came down to this: they would be happier if I left. And I would be too.

Knowing when to quit is a tricky thing. We often talk about quitting in a negative way: admitting defeat or giving up or selling ourselves short. But sometimes, quitting is courageous. Sometimes, it's about self-care and self-empowerment and choosing the better path for you. Sometimes, quitting is the very key you've been looking for to unlock the most stubborn door—the door that leads to greater contentment.

Happiness is a value that many people overlook for a number of reasons: perhaps because it seems so fleeting or excessive; perhaps because of a sense of undeservedness or unworthiness; perhaps because the rest of life's priorities seem to diminish the need or want for simple pleasure. A lot of people get so ingrained in their work, their pattern, or their history that they never look up. They never ask themselves, *Am I happy doing what I'm doing? Could I be happier doing something else?* I think the real question, beneath all of these other ones, is *Do I deserve to be happy?*

You see, I don't think we are supposed to be sad and depressed. I don't believe we're here to live a life of drudgery. I believe we're here to be happy and to live enriching lives, for ourselves and for others. At the firm, I was unappreciated and

I was very unhappy. Those guys didn't fully grasp investment banking (and justifiably so—they were accountants), and they were also unwilling to embrace a new way of doing things. Therefore, I would never be able to thrive in that environment.

There was no way around this truth, no way for me to rearrange the puzzle pieces to make myself fit, and therefore, I needed to get out. It was inevitable. I could have waited around for someone else to initiate this shift and simply kick the can (the decision) down the road. But I knew that the change would have to happen, whether it was right then or two years later. But what was the point of forcing it to work or dragging it out if I wasn't happy doing it?

There are many things we have to do in life that just aren't fun. But if we're spending eight or twelve hours a day doing something that makes us miserable, yikes. Why should anybody be miserable? And what can we do to change it? This requires an honest conversation.

Maybe happiness hasn't been an objective for you. I want to challenge you to think about your happiness as a goal worth chasing. The great (and tricky) thing about happiness is that it's always changing. It *is* fleeting. You can be happy for a moment, and then wake up and reevaluate—*what am I going to do today that will contribute to my happiness? How about tomorrow? And the day after that?*

I'm a big proponent of writing things down. I've told my kids for years, "If you can't find the words and write it down on paper, then you probably haven't thought about it enough. And it's not likely to happen." Take some time to put pen to paper and answer a few honest questions about your happiness:

- Are you happy?
- Does your life feel fulfilling?
- What makes you happy?
- What can you change to bring about more happiness?

Chapter 11

WHAT ARE YOU DOING HERE?

I WAS MORE READY THAN EVER to start my own firm, but once again, this plan was derailed—this time by a phone call from Stephen Albrecht, a prominent lawyer, trusted friend, and business advisor. A client of his needed help, he told me. Could I do for him what I had done for Levitt? It could be an exciting opportunity. I said that I wouldn't agree to working for the guy over the phone, but I would certainly go and meet him over breakfast.

He said, "OK, Covington Country Club, 7:00 a.m. Saturday. You're a member, aren't you?"

I said, "No, I'm not a member of the Covington Country Club."

I met Stephen as we were walking into the building, and we entered the dining room together. The first thing I noticed was that the place was almost entirely empty. *Had Stephen asked to have everyone cleared out for our privacy?* The next thing I noticed was a man sitting alone in the corner. This was Ward Streeter, Stephen's client. As we shook hands, it occurred to me that this was the car guy whose face I had seen on billboards around town.

I told Ward up front, "I don't really know anything about the car business, and I have to be honest—I don't know what you would expect me to do in the car business."

"What I want to talk to you about," he said, "has got nothing to do with car dealerships. I want to build an automobile fleet finance company."

I said, "Tell me more."

I learned that the typical car rental company operates as a franchisor. The retail locations at airports or offsite are then owned and operated by franchisees. These typically small franchise businesses couldn't get their cars straight from the auto manufacturers. The federal government wouldn't allow big fleet companies to go to the manufacturers and buy cars at a discount. Instead, the car rental companies had to go through a third party.

Ward said, "I'm going to be that third party, but I need a really big line of credit to do it."

Each individual car manufacturer (like Chrysler, Ford, or Honda) has a finance company. Ward's idea was very interesting: he wanted to figure out if there was a finance company that would enable him to buy all sorts of cars that he could then lease out to the franchisees of Alamo, National, Dollar, Thrifty, Fox, etc. And this idea sounded right up my alley. After some careful due diligence, I said, "Yes. Let's do it!"

And, once again, I put off starting my own business.

RUNAROUND

On my first day of work with Ward, I made my way into his headquarters, where his secretary greeted me with a bewildered look.

"What are you doing here?" she asked.

I said, "I'm the new guy working for Ward on the new fleet business. Gregory Smith, at your service."

She said, "Well, he's in the hospital and you're supposed to be there. Didn't he tell you?"

I thought, *Hospital? What the hell happened?* And no, he obviously hadn't told me.

It took me quite a while to drive to the hospital on wintery, snow-covered roads, where Ward was recovering from a small surgery, comfortably set up in one of the hospital's suites (suites I didn't know existed).

When I walked into his room, he also gave me a bewildered look. *Why is everyone so surprised to see me?* I wondered.

"Why are you here?" Ward demanded.

"It's my first day of work, and your secretary informed me that I was supposed to be here. So here I am."

He said, "You're supposed to be in Los Angeles."

"What am I supposed to be doing in Los Angeles?" I asked.

"I've got a big fleet of cars trapped in one of the national car rental companies. It's been turned over to receivership in bankruptcy. Someone was supposed to call and tell you to go meet with the bankruptcy trustee, Phil Jeffers."

I said, "Well, Ward, no one called me."

"I need you to figure out a plan to protect our financial interest," he said.

I thought, *How the hell am I going to figure that out?*

He said, "You can figure it out on the plane. The pilots have been waiting for you for two hours back in the city, at the airport."

I called my wife on my way to the tarmac and asked if she would pack me a bag and meet me there. I was on my way to Los Angeles, and I didn't know how long I would be there.

By the end of the week, I had concluded that maybe Ward Streeter should consider buying the car rental company. There was a lot of hidden value on the balance sheet. I spent the next couple of months in New York (since he had a plane and had told me to use it) initiating meetings with several private equity firms that backed big deals. And I presented the opportunity to acquire this big car rental company with Ward's trapped cars inside of it, a plan that would improve the balance sheet by several hundreds of millions of dollars.

One of the firms loved this idea so much that they sidestepped us and acquired the Los Angeles-based car rental company without Ward. They put an end run on us, and Ward was absolutely furious. While there was nothing we could do about it, I did go back and ask the New York firm if Ward could participate in the acquisition and invest in the company. They agreed. Today, this company is one of the largest car rental companies in the US. The New York equity firm that we engaged ended up selling the company for a fortune in about three and a half years (over twice what they had invested).

SUSPICION

By the time he got to know me, Ward had me doing all kinds of things. On top of getting the fleet company up and running, I was helping to facilitate the purchase of more car dealerships and working directly with managers of the car dealerships. While Ward owned many dealerships, from what I could tell, they didn't make a lot of money. And I found myself surrounded by a rather strange business culture—there were wacky things going on all of the time.

I tried to get access to certain financial information about the dealerships because they didn't make or lose much money but somehow always had plenty of cash. When I asked the man who was responsible for the cash flow at the corporate office, he was immediately defensive and snippy with me—"What do you need that information for? What does that have to do with your job? Did Ward ask you to talk to me?"

When I explained that the financial statements were unclear, that I wanted to know more, he would tell me to speak with Ward.

"No need for you to worry about that," Ward told me. "I've got it covered. We just need to make more money in the car dealerships."

When I tried to intervene with the general managers of the car dealerships, to offer some ideas to make more money, Ward asked me not to be so hard on them. When a sales manager came in who had lost confidence in his selling abilities, Ward would pump him up, send him out for a new custom-made suit, and say, "You can do it!" He gave every manager a company car to drive, and not just any old company car—a jacked-up, chromed-out ride of his choice. If he had a manager's meeting at our office, it was like a car show in our parking lot. And it all felt like one giant, manufactured spectacle.

Maybe this is just the car business, I thought. Or not.

On top of that nonsense, I could never meet with Ward alone, and I did find this incredibly bizarre. I would extend an invitation to meet at his favorite restaurant, assuming he was maybe uncomfortable talking business at the office with all the interruptions. But by the time I would arrive, there would be ten or fifteen people sitting at the table. I wondered, *Why won't the guy meet with me alone? What's up?*

Ward himself was very, very charming. He could sell almost anything to almost anyone. But he had a short fuse, particularly when it came to budget deficits or change-of-management conversations. If anyone ever suggested firing one of his general managers, his response was always the same: he absolutely blew his stack. "Nope, no way," he'd say. "We're not gonna let him go. He's a good guy. We'll put him back together again. He'll be selling more BMWs in no time!"

I didn't witness anything outright illegal, but the lack of accountability was alarming. Ward accepted strange behavior from his management team—people missing budgets without explanations, ignoring goals, apologizing over and over again—without dishing out any consequences. "Get out there and do a better job and you'll be fine," he'd say. I was accustomed to running businesses based on the numbers, on deliverable *results*, which required a great deal of accountability. But he didn't want to do that. My instinct: if people aren't holding each other accountable, it's likely a sinking ship. Ward was generous, maybe to a fault.

In all of this, one thing was very clear to me: I needed to keep my distance. He would tell me to take the keys to a Ferrari, and I would tell him, "I don't want to drive the Ferrari. I don't even know how to drive a Ferrari." (I figured out why I shouldn't be driving a Ferrari when I parked it at a business appointment one morning and couldn't figure out how to put it in reverse. I had to call Ferrari to find the reverse button!) I was skeptical, and in my gut, I felt these "gifts" maybe came with a hook.

GET THE JOB DONE

I did what Ward asked me to do and helped him build his fleet business to incredible levels in just a few years' time. I knew that Kia had recently bought an interest in Hyundai and that this might be a good place to start, so I put together credit facilities with a contact on the board of directors, and after a few months, we got a huge credit facility to get Ward's business to a new level.

We figured out a business model that would maximize profit, based on peak seasons. You see, if you rent a car from, say, Alamo, you're really renting from the guy that owns that particular Alamo franchise. Let's call him Joe. Joe, who owns a franchise in Tampa, can only get three hundred cars through Alamo because his balance sheet is itty bitty—he's just one tiny, little agency. But the thing is, Joe could easily lease three thousand cars in Tampa during peak season, when everybody flocks to Tampa in the wintertime.

So we figured out a way to ladder in these cars during prime times. If it was Denver, we'd load up the franchise in October and November for ski season, and then start pulling the cars out in March and April. Where would the cars go? Straight to auction at Manheim or Odessa.

But this posed another problem: after purchasing the cars from a manufacturer, leasing them out for five months, and selling them at auction, we would still owe a few thousand dollars on the car loan from the finance company. So we asked the manufacturer to pick up any shortfall from the auction sale to pay off the loan. In exchange, we offered reasonable assurance that we would continue to purchase a whole bunch more cars from them. They agreed because—while they would face an immediate loss—they knew the profit from the previous sale to us would ultimately balance out the loss, one quarter after another. They didn't just agree to it—they loved it.

Boy, did I have a lot of fun setting up this finance operation. It made a ton of money, and Ward paid me well and always treated me fairly and with respect. We built a great big fleet finance company with tens of thousands of cars. I mean, we'd order thousands of automobiles with one phone call and put them all over the place, and Ward became one of the largest automobile wholesalers in the country for several years.

EXIT PLAN

After my failed attempts at understanding the financial aspects of Ward's operation, I made the decision to stay in my lane. I would work on the fleet leasing business and steer clear of the rest. My intuition was that there was something unusual going on, and in the end I didn't want this to reflect on me. My reputation, integrity, and credibility were potentially on the line. An odd series of events had turned into a hunch and then into a deeper gut feeling. There wasn't anything blatantly obvious, but my sixth sense had been triggered. It was time for me to listen to my gut. Sometimes, it's easy to ignore these kinds of suspicions. Sometimes, reality just isn't fun to face. Sometimes (like me), you just want to finish what you started. I chose to complete the mission I had committed to and move on.

I reached out to a large leasing company, whom I had previously leased aircraft from (for Vacation Air) and got in touch with their automobile fleet leasing executives. It didn't take long to engage them in an exploratory discussion about buying Ward's unique fleet leasing business. Soon thereafter, we closed the deal and it put a big check in Ward's pocket. He was set for life, along with his next several generations, if he chose it. I was happy for Ward that this big payday had finally arrived.

I gave Ward a ninety-one-day notice of my departure and proceeded to work every one of those ninety-one days, almost exclusively on the sale. I had hired some solid folks to replace me and had them on board and trained. The deal didn't close until a few weeks after I left, but I continued to work to get it to the finish line. On my last day in the office, before boarding a flight to Nevada to meet with Rick Hamilton to start the next chapter in my career (I couldn't get out fast enough), Ward was begging me not to go. He offered me big bucks to stick around, but I had done what I was hired to do and it was time—I didn't want to be around for what may come.

A KEY: INTUITION

Question: If you can't be certain, will you trust your instincts?
Years after my time working for Ward Streeter, he was indicted over some financial matters that thankfully I knew nothing about. I thought he was on easy street when I left, financially set for life. Perhaps he protected me from the worst of it by discouraging me from asking questions and digging in because others went down with him, perhaps people who were enamored with momentary reward and fancy titles. It created a false sense of security and a false sense of success, and ultimately led to utter destruction.

How would you feel if your employer offered you a bunch of money, not for what you've done but for something you'll do in the future? Sound tempting? I mean, who doesn't want a big chunk of change in their pocket—right now? Your ego can go wild thinking about all you would do, who you would be. There's nothing wrong with money or having lots of it (I hope you do have lots of it, over time), but how you get it and what you do with it matters for the rest of your life. It determines who you are. Ask yourself, *How am I going to feel about this down the road? What are the potential consequences of this decision? Can I live with those?*

Thankfully, I had listened to my gut and kept my distance where appropriate. I knew there was something off about the appearances, and I didn't want to immerse myself too deeply. I kept my head down and stuck to my knitting. I worked hard for Ward, I achieved the expected results, and he was always fair to me. When I was asked to give testimony, it was by phone and only once—the authorities never came back to talk to me again. At that moment, I was incredibly thankful that I listened to that sixth sense.

Sometimes, your intuition is spot on. Then, the question becomes: what are you going to do about it? Are you going to put your own integrity on the line? Can you stick around and try to understand it or fix it? Are you going to take the payout? Keep your mouth shut? Or do you need to abort, call it quits, and move on?

We all want to trust people, to believe that people are good and honest, that they will tell us everything we need to know to fully understand and make informed decisions. But this simply isn't always true. At times, we have to rely on our own senses, our own gut feelings. That's why self-awareness is such an important tool in evaluating situations and people. And it's your duty to yourself to be self-aware. When you walk away from a conversation or an experience, notice how it makes you feel. Do you feel peaceful, assured, and informed? Or do you feel suspicious? Uneasy? Anxious? These feelings—this sixth sense—are sometimes all we need to avoid trouble and hardship. You have a gut. Trust it.

Chapter 12

ICEBERG, RIGHT AHEAD!

IT WAS EARLY 2005 when I decided it was time to part ways with Ward Streeter. I was planning on picking up where I left off with BANCO Advisors before the previous detour of duty. In the meanwhile, my wife and I had expanded our equestrian operation, and we owned and operated an eighty-acre ranch, where she was breeding Morgan horses and I was handling "the crops."

It was a Sunday morning in February and we had just gotten home from church. I went out to the barn and hooked up the manure spreader to our blue New Holland tractor and headed out to the snow-covered soybean fields to spread a load of horse poop (somebody had to do it!). As the white fields turned brown, I was listening to Garrison Keillor's talk show on the radio when my cell phone rang. It was Rick Hamilton!

"What are you doing, Greg?" Rick asked.

I said, "I'm emptying the manure spreader, Rick."

He said, "I want to know how things are going."

"In what context?" I asked, wondering if I should give him a play-by-play of my farming activities or a full rundown of my latest physical exam.

"Well, you know, I started this new bank," he said. "And I've expanded it into several states. And I have a lot of employees now."

"How many?" I asked.

He said, "Two-thousand. I'm in over twenty states and I've turned a $50 million investment into $500 million of capital without even taking a penny out. Greg, my daughters will eventually run the business, but not quite yet, and as you know them both, I'm calling you. We need some help, and I'd like you to come down here and take a look at it and think about joining us. You can pick a title and we'll work out a compensation package. How about CFO? And you can get on the board of directors."

I said, "I'll be there in the morning."

FIX IT

I had breakfast with Rick in Las Vegas the next day, where he described his vision of the bank and its future, but he also explained a very delicate problem that he was facing in Seattle, Washington. He was dealing with some new bank regulators that were all spun around and confused because of a bizarre conversation that his Seattle bank president had recently had with the regulators about the application and bank formation business plan.

Rick said, "Greg, I just need you to go there and fix this."

So, a few months later, I found myself en route to Rick's headquarters in Las Vegas, where I would be Rick's new CFO. The bank in Seattle hadn't yet opened its doors, but Rick had the building and infrastructure in place, had selected the board of directors, and had hired and trained employees. They were just waiting on bank regulatory approval. Rick had invested a great deal of money on forming the bank, but the regulators were dragging their feet because of some relatively minor inconsistencies in the regulatory application.

Come to find out (*after* I had accepted my position and moved myself to Las Vegas), there was a previous phone conference where Rick had gotten a little excited. It was reported to me that on this call—with several different regulators and several of Rick's bank executives—Rick confirmed his intention to change the business plan. This didn't sit well with the regulators. Rick ranted, "Why do you care? It's a more sound financial plan and we're going to do it. It'll be fine, so what's your problem?"

Well, the regulators didn't appreciate his tone and told Rick that they were going to issue a cease and desist order on the bank in Seattle. It wasn't even open yet! Now, Rick had already invested lots of money into this new operation. He wasn't going to go down that easily, and he was absolutely furious. Needless to say, Rick had a bit of a temper, and when the call ended, he proceeded to let everyone in the room know exactly how he felt, with several expletives sprinkled in.

Rick had good reason to be upset with the regulators. He had previously built several successful financial institutions, was operating one of the highest-performing banks in the country, and was a highly respected businessman (he still is, today). His employees were loyal to him and committed to his vision of building a highly profitable and sustainable national banking platform. Rick was equally loyal to his employees and the customers of the bank. The same regulators who were criticizing him had previously published their praise of him for his success in building a highly diversified bank. It was almost unbelievable that they would make such a big deal over the business plan issue, given Rick's incredibly successful history in what we know to be a highly regulated industry. But regulators have egos too!

WHAT I DIDN'T KNOW

Two weeks later, Rick received a subpoena for all of the documents related to the application—the organization's formation, operation plans, business strategy, etc. Rick, still reeling from this angry phone call, decided to give them *everything*, including Post-It Notes and over three thousand documents. He asked his secretary to type up the transcription from the conference call with the regulators, so she pulled out her headphones and got to work. He included that gem as well. Then, he shipped a pile of boxes in a FedEx truck to the regulators in Washington DC.

Upon receiving this truckload of paperwork, the regional director reportedly called Rick and said, "Rick, we got thousands of documents from you. We are not very happy about this, but I suppose you complied with the court order on the subpoena. Did you look at the documents you sent me?"

He said, "We sent every document that we had, just the way the subpoena read."

She said, "Yes, but did you *look* at every document?"

He said, "No, I didn't look at every document. I've got people that work for me that do that sort of thing."

"Well, Mr. Hamilton, the reason I'm asking you this question," she said, "is because there's a typed transcription of a phone conversation with us that you apparently recorded."

"Yes," he said, "I did record it. And now the terrible way you people treated me on the phone is on the record."

"Mr. Hamilton," she said, "I'd like you to read from the end of the transcript. After our phone call ended. Where you carried on and called me an a**! And you called the director of supervision a s***. And you threatened to call the attorney general of the United States. And then you go on to say something about burning in hell."

Rick's secretary had typed up the *entire* transcript, including Rick's infuriated tirade to his team after the call had ended. Right then and there, he grabbed his dictaphone and hurled it out the door of his office. And that's when he had made his call to me. I can't say that it all played out that way, but that's what I was told once I came on board.

VOTING NO

I could see the problem from the very beginning. Rick was dictating when he could have been listening and negotiating. He was highly intelligent but sometimes got on the defensive side of things quickly, combining threats and rage with what may have seemed like an unhealthy attitude. He took some things personally and lost perspective. Honestly, he likely could have solved this problem himself with a bit of humility, patience, and some deep breaths (maybe lots of deep breaths), by actually taking the time to listen, and by simply offering an apology for what seemed like a misunderstanding. But his ego may have stepped in front of him, and now the regulators had control.

After coming on board, I learned that half of the bank's employee base, about eleven hundred people, were purchasing and booking what were called "Alt-A subprime mortgages" from mortgage lenders and loan originators across the country. (These were later known as junk loans or liar loans based on a borrower's "stated income.") The bank paid its mortgage teams big bucks in incentives to get these loans on the books, even though many of these were issued to bizarrely underqualified applicants that would never be able to make payments and subsequently defaulted. This later unfolded (in 2008) as the story of empty homes all over the country filled with vagrants and alligators swimming in green pools, when thousands of homeowners quickly discovered that they could not afford the mortgage payments and gave their deeds back to the lenders, in lieu of foreclosure. But in the early 2000s, the federal government allowed banks to underwrite and fund these loans.

This business would become the bane of the whole banking industry and, in 2007, triggered the failure of Washington Mutual (the largest bank failure in history), IndyMac, and dozens of lending institutions. Rick's bank was right in the middle of this national financial debacle aggregating Alt-A mortgages from originators, letting them accumulate on the bank's balance sheet, and then selling them to the various securities houses on Wall Street. Ultimately, Lehman Brothers was sucked into this when bonds they sold, backed by these Alt-A subprime loans, defaulted. The economy as we knew it was wrecked. (Check out the movie *The Big Short* for a deeper understanding.)

After I realized the volume of Alt-A loans the bank was collecting and selling to Wall Street firms (we're talking billions of dollars), I confronted Rick and the board of directors and very plainly voiced my concern. While this activity had led to record-breaking profits for the bank over the previous years, and while bank regulators were encouraging other banks to consider this brilliant "model of diversification," it was clear to me that the system was innately broken (why it wasn't apparent to everyone else around me will forever be a mystery).

Loans originated and based on "stated income" were too good to be true for borrowers who would soon find out they couldn't afford their mortgage. The homes were almost entirely leveraged. Income wasn't verified. Hello?! What's wrong with this picture? It didn't take a lot of digging to understand that people would start missing payments and defaulting on their loans. The lines were going to cross. The premium bids the bank was accustomed to receiving would turn negative when credit quality was examined. Rick could ultimately lose the bank.

But...alas! The bank was making tons of profit and the sales teams were making lots of money off of these commissions, and no one was going to be deterred by my voice. I even brought in some of the leading bank advisors in the country, who offered the same advice: "Get out of the Alt-A business." The majority of the board chose to appease Rick, maybe stroking his ego, but they had no money at risk. I was nearly the only person on the board who voted to wind down the mortgage operation or sell it, and this went on for over a year.

At this point, it would have been easy to leave. I could see that a financial disaster was probably ahead of us. But I was certain that I could stick around without risking my reputation and integrity, to help Rick with the aftermath. I had voted no; there was a written record of my dissension. And I knew, when shit hit the fan, Rick was going to need some help, though he had done nothing wrong. At the end of the day, Rick was a great guy, a man that I respected and still do today, and a true friend to me. I felt pretty certain he was making the wrong bet on the economy, but I wasn't willing to abandon him, especially foreseeing what was to come.

STOP THE BLEED

Sure enough, eventually, a bid came in on a $300 million pile of mortgages at 92 percent, and automatically the bank was facing a $24 million loss. And then this same bidder, after doing their due diligence, readjusted their bid to $256 million—a $44 million loss! All of a sudden, a waterfall broke loose and it was never ending. I told Rick, "We should get out of this business right now. We have to do something else."

I suggested an orderly transition: there were competing subprime mortgage companies that would have bought the operation, maybe keeping eleven hundred people employed and maybe saving Rick's investment.

He said, "No, we can fix this. I'll put more money in and cover the losses. And by the way, Greg, you're taking over part of the mortgage operation."

I said, "No, thank you."

Instead, he named someone else to head up the mortgage operation, but it never got any better. Ultimately, the regulators came and seized Rick's bank and made an example out of one of the largest privately owned banks in the country. Rick was asked to stand down and the regulators auctioned off his banks—allegedly over a $2 billion loss. The feds are surely not the most effective auctioneers, but a loss was inevitable.

After it was all done, Rick Hamilton was featured in the *Wall Street Journal*, in a short article about the failure of the bank. At the end of the article, Rick talked about the regulators and about subprime mortgages and all that. The author asked him, "What are you going to do next, Rick?"

And he said, "I think I'm going to go sailing."

The article ended there. He didn't call the regulators a bunch of names or wallow in his self-pity. Rick was able to own his decisions and move on, and this was a perspective I greatly appreciated at the time.

A KEY: LOYALTY

Question: Who will you be true to?

At any point in this process, I could have left. I foresaw this bleak outcome long before it came to fruition, and Rick, for the most part, stuck to his alternative point of view. Most people probably would have left. Who wants to go down with a sinking ship?

So why did I stick around? It's a question I've pondered quite a bit. For one, by the time I realized the extent of this doomed operation, I was already wedded to the problem. I was an executive in the organization. I was a member of the board. I didn't feel like I could simply turn a blind eye. That also didn't mean I had to agree with it or like it or champion it. In truth, I was most committed to offering, in my view, a voice of reason in the midst of the chaos.

If you disrespect yourself, you're probably not worthy of being a friend to someone else. If you aren't proud of who you are, convicted in your beliefs, and willing to take a stand, you probably can't build an honest relationship based on integrity with another person. It was this pride, conviction, and devotion that allowed me to stand by Rick in the oncoming storm. I never once stopped telling him that he needed to get the hell out. I never once swallowed my own certainty and honesty for the sake of stroking his ego or making my life easier. I was loyal to myself, first and foremost.

I also stayed because of loyalty to Rick because he had honored his commitment to me with a great job that provided lots of challenges and problems that needed to be fixed. He tried to personally cover the bank's losses, didn't pay himself a salary, and didn't take anything. He was trying to build a thriving organization and a legacy for his daughters and loyal employees. He didn't do anything wrong. He was a good man that simply bet on the wrong side of the economy (he truly believed the market would correct itself and these mortgages were a sound investment). It didn't matter who was right or wrong. I genuinely wanted to help Rick because he was my friend.

When everything blew up—having spent twenty previous years managing and buying banks and working with regulators— I knew there was no place to hide. Rather than get stressed and lose control of myself, I decided to try and do what I could to manage a better outcome. I stayed on with the bank and helped with the transition after Rick was ousted, working with the regulators to recover losses and consider multiple recovery options.

I was able not only to garner favor with the regulators but to provide helpful information and advice. It was a way for me to help and stay true to Rick and to myself.

For me, loyalty is much broader than friendship or family or some elusive business hierarchy. I feel committed to every person involved in a problem that I am assigned to fix. Truly solving a problem involves looking at it from several vantage points. In this case, there were numerous people wrapped up in this subprime mortgage business and on a national level. It had become an industry to itself. I had to think about the officers, the employees, all the families, vendors, and of course the shareholders, the bank regulators, and the investors who had bought the bonds from Wall Street that were backed by the junk mortgages. Any recovery I could muster would help to defray all of these losses.

Our loyalty to certain beliefs, hopes, and desires can create tremendous success. Our loyalty to these same things can ultimately destroy us. One of Rick's daughters was originally heading up most of the lending operation. This was a big motivator for Rick to keep it running—he wanted his daughter to be successful, to be groomed to take over the business, and this was a solid training ground. Rick may have been blinded by loyalty to family and employees as the economy began to dramatically and quickly shift. We all have to learn what to be loyal to and when to cut ties.

Chapter 13

A WORKOUT BUDDY

DURING MY TIME WITH Rick Hamilton, Jack, an old friend and former partner from the CPA firm I had worked at, asked if I would meet with a young buck he knew from Albuquerque, the son of a rug merchant that he had recently become friends with.

"This kid needs some help," Jack told me. "He'll be in Las Vegas next week, moving in with his father, and he may need a little mentoring."

Now, I was trying to manage a big privately owned bank and a business that was starting to spiral out of control, but I owed Jack a favor. And I respected him—he was a kind, caring person—so I simply couldn't say no. Anyways, amidst the chaos that was unfolding at the bank at the time, I figured I could use a little distraction. So I told Jack, sure, I'd meet with the kid. Send him to our corporate offices, I told him.

That day, security pinged me, "There's a kid here to meet with you, Greg. And frankly, he just looks strange. What should we do with him? Should we tell him to go away?"

I said, "No, send him up to the boardroom."

BEYOND APPEARANCES

This boardroom was enormous. I had to wrap up a few phone calls and business items before I could meet with him. So this poor kid found himself alone at a mile-long table that could sit over fifty people, in the corporate offices of our banking headquarters. This was undoubtedly out of his comfort zone. It would have scared the pants off any normal nineteen-year-old kid. But not Kasim Aslam.

When I finally entered the boardroom, I was quite literally shocked by this guy's appearance. He was a six-foot-four Pakistanian, all skin and bones, with dark hair pulled into a long ponytail, and a long, black leather coat, looking like he had just dropped straight out of the movie *Matrix*. Come to find out, he was dabbling in acting and modeling at the time and was hoping to get a mortgage for a house, but no one was taking him seriously. Well, I couldn't see why!

I was recovering from a shoulder injury at the time, and rather than be on a morphine drip for six months, I opted for a six-month rigorous physical therapy program. I was hitting the gym three mornings a week, usually starting at oh-dark-thirty. That evening over dinner, I asked Kasim if he maybe wanted to join me at the gym the next morning. He was skinny as a rail, and I thought maybe—mentoring aside—I could at least help him put some meat on his bones.

He said, "How early?"

I said, "How about I pick you up at 5:30?"

And he—or should I say his twenty-year-old ego?—said, "Well, how about 5:15?"

And I, thinking, *I can play this game*, said, "Well, OK, how about if I pick you up at 5:00 then?"

And he said, "Well, I could be ready at 4:30."

So I picked him up at 4:30 the next morning, and I started teaching him correct form for lifting weights. I also thought that maybe if he got fit, he'd quit smoking three packs of cigarettes a day too (a strange trend that hadn't yet gone out of style in Albuquerque). Along the way, I even hired a trainer—Carter Gibson—to really amp up our exercise regimen. We were going to get fit! And this was the start to a lifelong friendship between me, a banker from Minnesota, and Kasim Aslam, a punk kid from Albuquerque.

After realizing that his acting aspirations were not really paying the bills, Kasim had decided that he wanted to start his own business. And the last thing he wanted was to be stereotyped as a rug merchant or work for his father, which of course he did for a while to pay some bills. So—obviously—I bought him some self-help books. Not because he was lacking confidence. No, Kasim Aslam *oozed* confidence. Truth be told, I thought that maybe he had *too much* confidence. But I could tell there was something fragile lurking inside of him, some deep questions beneath all of this self-assurance: *Can I really do this? Do I have what it takes?* But on the outside he could conquer anything.

I had noticed that in many situations, he would almost apologize for not having the necessary experience or a college education. After all, his "credentials" included petty street crimes, owning quite a few guns, and living in his father's basement. He certainly didn't know how to form a business, how to engage with clients, or how to invite someone into a professional conversation. He didn't even know what a salad fork was!

But man—he was brilliant. And street smart. And maybe more than anything, he was eager to learn and experiment on his own.

He read every professional self-help book out there, listened to me share my experiences over multiple drinks and dinners, and then began crafting his own unique ideas about the formation of a new business.

But there was something *big* standing in his way. Kasim had this way of circling back to his upbringing as a disadvantaged kid in Albuquerque, having to assist with the care for his divorced and single blind mother and younger brother. He had some real struggles growing up, and it was incredible that he had made it as far as he had, but I could tell he felt stuck—not only in that city but in his identity as the underdog, in his perceived lack of resources, in his fear of limited horizons for the rest of his life.

We all have to face our limitations at some point. It can be our background or upbringing, our lack of skills or education, our insecurities or fear or guilt or you fill in the blank. Sometimes these constraints are real and haunting, sometimes they may be insurmountable, and only you can determine what's true. For Kasim, I could tell that his limitations were mostly a matter of perspective. He needed to start seeing himself differently, to understand his value, and to learn how to use his personality, experiences, and skills to his advantage. And I was not about to let him slide back to Albuquerque either!

GIVE A LITTLE

My answer to this dilemma was inviting him to join us on a family trip to Egypt. I thought maybe he needed to see the world, get outside of his own picture of hopelessness, expand his horizons. Honestly, I wanted him to see true, abject poverty, to witness firsthand people starving in the streets without access to food, medicine, or resources: the worst of the worst conditions. I wanted him to see the bad and the ugly of life, with the hope that he could shift how he saw his own life and opportunities. Plenty of people have risen from the poorest streets of Egypt, Africa, and many developing countries.

You might think how bizarre—how random—to take this kid to Cairo. As it turned out, my family (and an entourage of about twenty people from the US) were headed to a wedding there.

I have several friends in political offices there and I had visited before. I knew it would be easy for Kasim to fit in with our crew but, more importantly, that he would see something far different from his own experiences. I knew that this *seeing* would be far more powerful and impactful than anything I could teach or tell him.

As hoped, this trip was exactly the kick in the pants that Kasim needed: he got his life in Albuquerque out of his head as he saw hundreds of people living in real, destitute poverty and realizing there were millions more. He realized that maybe he wasn't limited by his past, that perhaps he had far more opportunities than he realized. Pretty soon, Kasim was living a life of gratitude. He was accepting who he was, and also *owning* it. He was starting to figure out how he could do better, rise up, become the person he dreamed of. After that, he really, really wanted to be successful in his business. He leveraged his skills and what he knew and became an acting coach. He stepped it up and upped his game.

Along the way, I learned that both Kasim and his younger brother were tested and scored with high Mensa scores, meaning they're both extremely intelligent (certainly more so than me). But Kasim had not yet experienced real success. He hadn't *felt* it. At that time, he was mostly feeling deep remorse for his lifestyle as a street punk in his earlier years and a deep desire to up his game and give something back to society.

I wanted Kasim to learn patience, to learn to listen to other people, to examine a situation, all for the sake of making better choices. I wanted him to see that if he could project where he wanted to be in a few years and commit to the process, he had everything inside of him to succeed. I wanted to teach him the lessons I'd learned during my life. His brain was now turned on to thousands of possibilities and running like a supercomputer, but he needed to take one step at a time. He needed a plan. And a bit of professional experience wouldn't hurt either.

So I decided to get him a cubicle and a desk at Rick Hamilton's Citizens National Bank, on the second floor, where the corporate offices were (this was before all of Rick's banks were auctioned off by the regulators). He was right smack-dab in the middle of all the action of our wholesale mortgage operation. He needed to hear people negotiating, selling, buying commercial transactions, talking about their families and the baseball game and simple life stuff. He hadn't done any of those things (he had been busy on the streets of Albuquerque doing who knows what?).

While everyone around him was hustling at Rick's bank, Kasim was tasked with launching his business. I helped him get a job doing some technology development work that led to a few successes and a few more successes, and eventually he started building his own technology company. His dad made some calls to his contacts in Lahore and Karachi, Pakistan, and soon Kasim had college-educated, well-trained support teams working on projects.

He learned how to lay down precise instructions. His teams, working twelve hours ahead in Pakistan, would execute on these instructions, so when Kasim awoke—voila!—work was done and ready to be reviewed. I introduced him to all sorts of people: guys in accounting, data processing, and the mortgage operation. They were all roughly the same age, and I told him he should have coffee and lunch with these guys. They could be his friends too.

People would come and ask me, "Who's that strange cat sitting in the middle of the mortgage operation? I thought security threw him out weeks ago."

I'd just smile and say, "Go find out for yourself. Go meet him."

It turns out, as people got to know him, they thought he was a pretty intriguing guy. I think he started to see himself differently, to understand that he brought a unique flavor to the room, that the very things that had felt limiting had actually made him an interesting human. He found out that he could think outside the box and figure things out way faster than most people. He discovered something that challenged all of his potential, and he took off.

I also bought him some shirts and trousers that actually fit, and told him to stick around for a while.

"Watch and see what happens around this mortgage operation," I told him. "You're eventually going to see this whole thing explode."

And of course he did—right up to two years later on a Friday afternoon at four o'clock, when fifty or more federal bank examiners showed up to seize the bank. He saw it all. So I'd like to think it was quite an accelerated grow-up-and-mature program for him.

GET A LITTLE

Much to my surprise, Kasim became a mentor to me in many ways as well. He certainly opened my eyes to things that I knew nothing about.

During this time, Kasim called me up one day and said, "gg, for all the things you've done for me, I want to give you a gift. And you can't reject it. I'm picking you up at six o'clock tonight so I can give you my gift."

So, Kasim picked me up and drove me across town to an acting studio, where I was greeted by Matt, a fellow acting coach of Kasim's and owner of the studio.

Matt said, "Kasim has bought you three acting lessons. Here's your script! And here are the other characters in the script. We're going to do a play and you're going to be in it!"

So I took the three lessons (because I had promised Kasim I wouldn't reject his gift), and then I went back for more lessons. Eventually I was even cast in a couple of short films as the token old, white guy. In one of them, I was a mobster and had to carry a pistol. Of course, I had never carried a gun before, and I was supposed to keep this thing in the back of my belt and effortlessly pull it out and shoot a guy like it was second nature. But every time I'd pull it out, the trigger would get stuck or the gun would be upside down or I'd just drop the dang thing.

Eventually Kasim and the director said, "Stop, stop, stop. Here's a rope—you're going to strangle the guy instead." Talk about solving a problem with innovation.

A KEY: CURIOSITY

Question: Do you judge a book by its cover?

There were so many moments in the beginning of my surprising friendship with Kasim that I could have walked away. There was absolutely no reason for me to say yes to addressing his challenges. I had no attachment, no obligation to this kid, and we had seemingly nothing in common. If I'm honest, I would have never thought that he had anything to offer me. Here was a nineteen-year-old wannabe street kid from a city I disliked quite a bit, who simply wanted me to sign off on a mortgage so he could feel like he was moving up in the world.

Why did I say yes? Why did I invest time in this kid? Because I saw tremendous potential and a hungry mind. Simply put, I was curious. What was Kasim capable of? What did he want to do with his life? How could I help him on his way?

What a shame if I refused to open a few doors for him. To invite him to engage all his senses so that he could, in time, unlock these doors himself. And he did. He set his ego aside and was willing to receive, completely and honestly. He became curious, and as a result, he became true to himself and to his potential.

At one point in time, everyone in Spain thought the world was flat. One guy thought maybe it wasn't, and his curiosity led to discovering that the world was, in fact, round. Curiosity is a superpower. One seemingly unimportant question can lead to the most brilliant discoveries. One rabbit hole can lead to an entire world of possibilities. One innocent meeting can lead to the most meaningful relationships.

I didn't know what I was saying yes to, in many ways. Relationships are like that: they can unfold like nesting dolls, a treasure inside of a treasure that just keeps surprising you with their color and beauty and uniqueness. And the best relationships are reciprocal—where you learn from each other, where you sharpen each other, where you open each other up to new experiences, ideas, and opportunities. That has been my experience with Kasim, and with many of my dearest relationships.

But true relationships require curiosity. We have to step outside of ourselves to explore and understand other people. For me at the time, a fifty-year-old investment banker, to invite a still-teenage cocky kid to come work out with me in the mornings—that was motivated by a number a of things: a true belief that every single person has something to offer, a deep curiosity about who this kid was and could be, and a desire to connect with people who are different than me. What a gift I found in Kasim. What I would have missed out on if I had chosen to be stingy with my time, to be close-minded, or to allow my ego to take the reins.

I am a firm believer that I do not know all the best answers. I certainly don't know everything. There are lots and lots of people who are smarter than me and far more interesting than me.

> I have found over my lifetime, both in business and personally, that some of the best ideas and the most significant introductions come from the most unlikely sources. We simply need to foster a spirit of curiosity, to seek to learn from and understand all that life throws our way.

Chapter 14

NEVER TOO LATE

AFTER RICK HAMILTON'S SHIP SUNK, I stayed on for another year at the request of the US Treasury Department to help Provident Insurance Company transition from insurance into banking. I wasn't required to do this, but it was the right thing to do, it turned out, the *smart* thing to do. Provident is one of the oldest insurance companies formed in the US, but at the time, they knew little about banking, and they had acquired certain parts of the bank. After this assignment, I formed a small boutique financial advisory firm with two influential and long-standing business guys in Phoenix, where I managed this firm for a few years.

Ultimately, this didn't quite feel like the right fit. They made the intros and I did all the work.

I thought to myself, *Did I really just endure forty years of incredibly hard but insightful work, figuring out solutions to all kinds of problems, if I had not been preparing myself to run my own business, for God's sake? I must have learned something along the way to mitigate the risk of starting my own business.*

I considered everything I had learned, all I had been through, the many hats I had worn, and I was pretty darn certain that I was ready to start an investment banking business of my own. A business about buying and selling businesses, consulting on businesses, fixing businesses, working with business owners, and helping them take their businesses to the next level.

So in 2012—thirteen years after wrapping things up with Levitt, and thinking it was time to start my own business—I finally did it. By that time, I had tons of valued relationships in Minnesota and the southwestern states, and thankfully had a pretty solid reputation as the guy who tried to save Hamilton's bank (instead of a guy who jumped ship or ran Hamilton's bank into the ground). With these connections and four decades of successful years in business, across multiple industries, I was confident that I could launch a successful financial advisory business. So, after renewing my securities license, I finally formed my very own financial advisory firm and named it BANCO Advisors (BANCO was the old ticker trading symbol of my first employer). My long-awaited plan of owning my own business was before me, and I would soon find out if I could make a living at it.

I think there are moments for anyone who decides to launch a business where they second-guess themselves. It was no different for me. I had worked for employers my entire adult life, and one day I woke up and realized, *I'm the employer.* There was freedom in this realization. And also, sheer terror! I had to write my own policy, my own script, my own future. I had to guard myself against my own fear of failure. I had to get up every morning and show up, not just hoping for the best, but *believing* that I would succeed. Knowing it, in my very depths. It was time for me to trust myself and feel confident doing so.

And, you know, people started calling me. It turns out that my experiences, my successes, maybe especially my failures running and managing businesses were relevant to them. The businesses I had run for other families and the problems I had solved were relevant to them as business owners. I could bring my experience and perspectives across most any industry and translate it into sound business advice. And get paid for it!

From the very beginning, it felt right. It felt like a beautiful culmination of all of my past experiences and my innate skills coming together. There were problems that needed fixing and that's the stuff I know how to do. It's something I feel in my bones. It's like a seventh sense. Almost always, fixing these problems involves sincere listening and then showing people that they often have the answers deep down inside of them. They know what to do; they just haven't articulated it or they are too fearful to take a step forward. Fear or ego may have taken hold. I get to listen, ask pertinent questions, translate their thoughts and goals into a plan, and offer actionable steps to create a pathway forward.

Soon enough, I had experienced a few wins. I don't mean money in my bank account, although that came too. I mean emotional wins. I felt like I had accomplished something great. That I had helped a business owner survive and ultimately thrive. That I was successful in my own right. I discovered that one of the most gratifying parts of owning a business was that I, too, was the beneficiary. I owned the outcomes I created. The gains, the successes, the celebrations—those were mine. I was accountable for my successes and failures. I owned them as I owned my business.

We all have a right to feel this way. We are meant to feel good about ourselves. To be successful and to feel some wins. To reap the rewards of our hard work. To figure out what we're good at, stick to our knitting, fine-tune our skills, and then, during our lifetime, give it all away.

PASS IT ON

A few months into running the new biz, I received a call from a former business partner. He said, "You know, you should have some help for all the work you do."

I was under the impression he was offering *his* help, and so I said, "I'm just fine. Thank you."

He said, "Will you take a meeting with someone?"

Having had this exact question put to me more than once (mostly always with interesting outcomes), I said, "Tell me more."

As he began describing this young man I would soon meet, I was immediately reminded of Kasim Aslam and knew that I needed to hear this guy out. Not because they were similar in any way (in reality, they had polar opposite backgrounds), but I had a feeling in my gut that this might just be an answer to a problem I had not yet identified. This kid was just out of college, with his securities licenses, and had had an unfortunate experience at a firm that blew up after eight months of him working there (the firm, not the young man). This kid was looking for work, and he was malleable and motivated. I didn't need the help right then, but I figured I might need some help down the road, especially if I wanted my business to truly take off.

I met Zachary at my office the following week and immediately had a feeling that there was something significant about our encounter. We talked for a while, I asked a lot of questions (as usual), and I listened. He had come from a very affluent background—both of his parents were well-known, respected doctors in town. And although he had been handed many opportunities in life, I sensed a drive in him, a desire to work hard, a longing to make a name for himself, rather than ride on the coattails of his parents. He wanted a fresh start where he could discover his potential.

TRIAL RUN

We never fully know what we are capable of, where we might excel, if we never try. Some of us never get a chance to figure this out. Some people get pushed or nudged in a certain direction or caught in a stereotype or influenced by others, stuck in a cycle of fulfilling other people's expectations and perhaps never really determining their own. My dad wanted me to go into the postal service. I had to fight that expectation, to risk disappointing my dad, and work hard to prove that the path I had chosen was viable, something to be proud of, something I could be good at on my own and because I had chosen it. Perhaps I saw a little bit of myself in Zach that day—a young man who was willing to say yes, to do the work, to take a chance, and to listen and learn.

I thought I could help him on the way, and so I asked him if he wanted to join me at a meeting with a bank client that same afternoon.

"We're just getting underway," I told him. "And you can be at the very front end of it. See it all. I'll introduce you as my associate. But don't get me wrong; I'm not paying you."

I was throwing this kid into the deep end, seeing if he'd float.

"Can you get a sports coat before two o'clock?" I asked him.

"Yes, I can," he said.

I gave him the address, told him to meet me there, and encouraged him to show up and ask questions and really engage.

This twenty-four-year-old showed up looking like a rock star or athlete in his fitted sports coat, asked some intelligent questions, and carried himself in a natural, confident way. I called him a few days later and asked him if he'd like to sit in on a meeting about a real estate project in a few weeks.

"It's going to need some fixing," I told Zach. "And we're gonna be the fixers. You wanna join me?"

He said, "Yeah, I do."

I gave him the address, and again, told him to meet me there.

And guess what! He did the work, created the selling memorandum, engaged with the client, was professional and insightful, and ultimately won me and the client over. The client remains a friend of ours to this day.

I said, "Would you like to work with me for a while? I'll give you an office and a desk, and we can share the coffee machine. But we're going to pay you based on our financial successes."

And again he said, "Yes!" Not, "How much?" or "What percentage?" He trusted me and that I would reward him.

SUCCESSION PLAN

Not long after Zach started working with me, he helped us experience some pretty big successes, so he got nice paychecks. And I said, "You know, if you think this is a relationship we can nurture, I'd like to start paying you a regular retainer."

And he said, "That sounds good to me."

So I started paying him every month, and he came in every day and took on more responsibilities. And at the beginning of 2021—eleven years after he started working with me—I sat down with him and said, "Zachary, I want you to consider running the firm. I can't manage all of it anymore. I've got kids and grandkids showing up at my lake house at 4:00 p.m. on Fridays, and I can't be on client calls and making my family wait for me to come out of my office to start the boat and the weekend."

He said, "I figured it was about time for me to do this." I loved hearing this!

I said, "Great. Everything that we do from here on out, we're 50/50 partners. You can carry any business card you want. It can say, 'King of England' or whatever you want. I think President would be perfect if that's OK with you".

And so Zach now runs BANCO Advisors, and I pop in here and there to advise or simply listen, but he's the man in charge now and a respected force to be reckoned with.

Zach maintains a cool demeanor and is a fantastic listener. He connects the dots faster than anyone in the room and never lets on that he is likely the smartest in the room. His ideas and innovations are well thought out and solid. He is a great leader.

OPENING DOORS FOR OTHERS

Not many people can say that they have had the opportunities to do as many things as I have done. I'm grateful for these experiences, and endlessly grateful for the people who helped open doors for me along the way. When I met Zachary—in the same way with Kasim—I saw an opportunity to open a door for this young man.

But here's the thing: it was his choice to walk through it or not.

And he did. He walked through the door, experienced success, and became a superstar. He took a risk with me, got out of his comfort zone, jumped in headfirst, and blossomed—opening and unlocking new doors all the time. And it was a win for me too. I got to cultivate and develop the person who became my business partner and would eventually take over my business. I never imagined my business practice would have a legacy. Now with Zach, its future is built on our solid foundation, working together, and he is free to proceed with his own vision as to how the future will unfold.

And this is the power of perspective and projection. From the very beginning, I saw so much potential in Zach: the type of person who could follow in my footsteps, lead with integrity, build our business, and bring new ideas and relationships to the table. But that wasn't a guarantee. I had to invest time and energy into him, with no guarantee that he would want the path I envisioned for him. I had to hold this hope loosely. But at the same time, I let Zach know that I believed in him and that I hoped he would fill my shoes in the future. In time, he has become a leader with his own vision of the future that I respect. I am on board with Zach. For me, this feels great.

BUILT ON RELATIONSHIPS

Do you know how many times I've advertised or run an ad or marketed my services?

Never. Not once.

Investment banking is generally all about transactions. Investment bankers don't have time for relationships because they are on to the next transaction. They have to create hundreds of thousands of dollars in fees for their firm.

This is never how I've viewed our business, perhaps because I've stood on the other side—I've stood in the shoes of my clients, the business owners. I've managed businesses across multiple industries, often regulated by the federal government. I've bought and sold businesses for my clients and for the families who trusted me to run their businesses. I've seen how money can breed all kinds of problems, how it can become a crutch, how debilitating it can be. I've also seen how much money can do for good and what can happen if we invest our time in relationships. Transactions follow and opportunities surely abound.

A KEY: VISION

Question: Do you believe in your powers of projection?

When I finally decided to launch BANCO Advisors, I had a lot of tools in my toolbox. The question was: What could I do with these tools? What could I build? A bridge? Or a skyscraper? Or a machine?

Our belief in ourselves and others unlocks incredible possibilities. When we believe we are capable of doing something, when we see ourselves living into this potential, it increases our chances of success. Furthermore, when we stop feeling limited by the fear of failure, we can function with more freedom and confidence. Mistakes are one of our greatest teachers, and while shame and embarrassment rear their ugly heads in these moments of perceived defeat, they are necessary for our development as humans. In order to reach our fullest potential, we have to reframe these shortcomings as opportunities for growth, as gifts we can learn from. We were never meant to be perfect. We are meant to always be expanding and becoming. But, in order to do this, we have to have vision—for ourselves and for our future.

When I started my business, I knew I wanted to see how far I could go. I knew I wanted to help others realize their potential, in the process of realizing my own. I wanted to take all of the knowledge and experiences I had collected and put them all together, to offer advice and knowledge for the benefit of others, and to continue to learn from new people and businesses.

Vision—for ourselves, for others, for our families or businesses or the year ahead—helps establish mile markers, checkpoints to hold us accountable: *Am I becoming who I hoped I would be? Is this choice moving me in the right direction? Do I want my family to be known for this? How does this change affect the people around me and my career goals?*

Vision also empowers the idea of projection. If I have a clear picture of who I want to be and what I want to be doing three years down the road, then I can make decisions with more clarity. If you're eighteen and know that you want to become a partner at a law firm someday, then your efforts and pursuits in undergraduate school should reflect this long-term goal. That's not to say that you need to know exactly where you're headed. After all I have learned, I firmly believe and embrace (and hope you do too) that our journey is our destination. Perhaps it's enough to have a vision of the person you want to be and live toward that: a person of integrity or kindness or passion. That's up to you.

This also applies to our family members, our friends, our coworkers, our bosses, and even the person bagging our groceries at the store. When we start to carry a vision for others, we unlock not only possibilities for them but possibilities for ourselves, our mutual investment into someone else's future. We have the great privilege of speaking into other people's lives, believing in them when they don't believe in themselves, painting a picture of what is possible and what they are capable of, without putting unnecessary pressure on them to become something they don't want to be. This requires a great deal of listening, tuning in to understand what they want for themselves. Helping others to find the courage to embrace choice and to move forward with their lives. Enabling them to dig down deep and find their own answers and to move forward with their vision, their journey.

Chapter 15

GETTING OLDER IN A LIVING WAY

WHEN MY SECOND GRANDSON, Everett, was just a toddler, I would walk through his front door and immediately he would jump up and say, "Grandpa gg, will you play with me?"

I would get down on my hands and knees and play cars and trucks or tear around the backyard and kick a soccer ball or read a book. Lots and lots of books. Now, at age eight, it's hard to find him without a pair of headphones on, buried in some three-hundred-page novel, or with a computer in front of him, designing digital games. He tells me all the time that someday he'll be the best game designer there is, and I have no doubt this will come to fruition.

This past summer, we spent the Fourth of July with my daughters and their families in northern Minnesota, along the shores of Lake Superior. There's a ski resort nearby that offers gondola rides and luge runs in the summertime.

Everett, in a rare moment, turned to me and said, "Grandpa gg, will you come down the luge with me?"

I was immediately taken back to that little three-year-old boy that used to ask me to play with him. So, of course, without thinking, I said, "Absolutely. You bet." I mean, what seventy-two-year-old would not want to launch himself down a mountain on a tiny-wheeled cart on a concrete half-pipe?

And that's how I found myself, a few moments later, side by side with Everett, gazing down two steep concrete tracks, atop a yellow, plastic sled that could not possibly be made for a grown man. I was told I could control how fast I would ride from top to bottom, that there was "no need for speed." All I needed to do was move the stick in front of me forward to go at lightning speed, or back to slow it down.

I got this, I thought to myself. *Forward, fast. Back, slow. Here we go.*

"It's a green light, Grandpa gg!" Everett said. "Let's go!!" (He had to tell me that because I can't tell the difference between red and green.)

We took off down the tracks—Everett on the left and me on the right—and I soon lost sight of my grandson and decided I needed to focus all of my efforts on survival. This was not the "choose your own adventure" I had anticipated. Every time I whipped around a bend, I sank into the middle of the track, only to be launched to the very top edge as I whipped back in the other direction. It wasn't long before I whipped right up and over that edge, rolling several times, and eventually coming to a painful halt on the gravel and grass that bordered the concrete track.

My knees and elbows had taken the brunt of the tumble, and I was immediately thankful it wasn't worse. I figured Everett was already at the bottom of the mile-and-a-half-long track, wondering what had become of his grandfather. I also knew someone was coming down behind me (and quickly), so I dusted myself off, got back on my wheeled sled, and made my way (a little slower than before) to the bottom, where Everett was waiting.

"You won that one," I told him as I stood up, blood dripping from my extremities.

"Grandpa gg," he said. "I didn't know what happened to you. This lady came down and said, 'There's some old guy that tipped over on the hill,' but I didn't think it was you. I don't think of you as an old guy."

"It was me," I said.

"Well, I'm glad you made it."

THE PROBLEM OF AGING

For most people, aging is an impossible problem. And I don't want to discount the real struggles of getting older: our bodies giving out, sickness, death of loved ones, chronic pain, the list goes on. Getting old can and often is problematic in so many ways, and I'm certainly not suggesting that you launch your aging body (or very young one for that matter) down a mountain like I did. For most people, this is just not a good idea (and clearly it wasn't a very good idea for me either).

What I do want to suggest is more of a shift in perspective, unlocking a different way to look at these later years of life that I'm currently living in.

A friend of mine called the other day and we were catching up on all of the things—work, grandkids, hobbies. He said to me, "Greg, you're one of the coolest cats I know. You're getting older in a living way."

That really touched me. In truth, it's something I've been thinking about a lot lately. What does it mean to get older in a living way? Whether you're twenty-two or eighty-nine, what does it look like to keep *living*?

Despite Everett's denial of my old age, I am getting up there in years. This is no more apparent than when I think about the number of funerals I've been to lately. Too many funerals. But I have to say, these celebrations of life have prompted me to think more deeply about this thing we call legacy—the things we pass on to the next generation, whether it's money or ideals, ethics, or faith. What example have I set, and what am I leaving behind?

Many of the funerals I have attended have been for people successful in business, people who have built companies, invented genius ideas, and made a bunch of money. But we're not talking about these things at their funerals. We're talking about how these individuals changed people's lives. About opportunities they created for others. About the impact they had on someone else's journey. About their investment and dedication to relationships: friends, employees, family, and sometimes even strangers.

I have four grandchildren who I collectively call the ACES because that's the acronym their initials make—Ava, Cooper, Everett, and Sebastian. And here's the thing: I don't want to just be "the old guy" to these four. I want to be their friend. Their advocate. Their confidant. I want to be the guy they call up and say, "Can we go get ice cream? Can we go to the mall? Can I talk to you about something?"

This goes back to something my folks ingrained in me, and that's self esteem—being confident, making choices, figuring out the right thing to do, and enjoying life. I want to be a person that instills these attributes into the ACES—not another parent or teacher or disciplinarian, but a person they can bounce ideas off of, engage in honest conversations with, and come to for advice.

Business taught me that enabling others to think for themselves and think about their own potential is far more important than balancing a balance sheet or closing a deal. I'm not particularly concerned about how I'm remembered, but I do want my grandkids to remember me as a helpful and loving guide on their journey, someone who encouraged them to consider all of life's endless, remarkable possibilities.

It's way more fun for me to show up in this way, to enable and empower their unique selves. That's why I traded my Corvette Stingray in for a tricked-out SUV that has lots of space in the back for hockey bags, riding saddles, ice skates, and soccer equipment. Most weekends you'll find me cheering on the ACES at the hockey rink, the horse-jumping arena, or the soccer fields. This season of life is about pouring into and showing up for them.

CARPE DIEM

One of the families that I worked for contributed a lot of money to the Lupus Foundation, where I got to meet the chairwoman at the time. Her name is Jenny Wold, and she herself is a Lupus survivor—an absolutely inspirational woman who organized, developed, and built the local chapter. She has faced many difficult days in her life—pain and suffering and so many unknowns—and these are the sorts of people that carry much hidden wisdom.

"What keeps you going?" I asked Jenny one day, as we were meeting in her office.

"Carpe diem," she replied, smiling.

"What does that mean?" I said.

She said, "It means seize the day. I think about it all of the time. We never know how much time we have, so I want to make the most of every day that I do have."

Looking at her office walls, I saw a couple of posters and signs with "carpe diem" or a similar sentiment written on them—her reminders to not quit, to give it her best shot, to show up and give back.

This has always stuck with me, this idea of seizing the day.

STAYING ENGAGED

I wake up each morning curious about what the day holds—who I'll talk to, what opportunities will arise, how the day will unfold. Truthfully, I *expect* something exciting and positive to happen. And it always does.

Many people expect the opposite. They get up in the morning having already decided that the day will be horrible. And inevitably, it is. We often get what we expect out of life. If I expect my days to be mundane or frustrating, I will find negative things to focus on. If, instead, I expect my days to be surprising and joy-filled, I am going to look for these things that will bring a smile to my face.

We're on different journeys, and therefore getting older looks different for each one of us. Unfortunately, we haven't found a cure for cancer or dementia or many other maladies that invade our bodies. There are many aspects of our day-to-day lives that we simply can't control. While we don't get to choose our DNA or health problems, we do get to choose to care for ourselves to the best of our abilities and resources.

I am deeply committed to keeping my mind and body as healthy as possible—for myself and for my loved ones (I don't want to be a burden on them later on). That's part of why I stay engaged with Zach and the business, why my wife and I became "reverse" snowbirds and returned to Minneapolis (to be closer to our kids and grandkids), and why I've tried to nurture my relationships over the years. I also hit the gym six days a week, and many afternoons you'll find me logging miles on my bike (unless it's wintertime in Minnesota—then I'm avoiding the roads altogether). These are ways I can contribute to my own mental and physical health so that I can stay active with the people and the things I love. So that I can wake up each day with gratitude and expectation. And—if (perhaps when) I ever do face serious illness—I'll be in the best shape possible to endure it.

FINISH THE JOURNEY

There are a few undeniable equalizers in life. One is the wait in line at the DMV. Another is death. Some say taxes is another, though I have seen some pretty clever workarounds on this front. However, I think time is the ultimate equalizer. When time has passed, it's irretrievable. It's simply gone. And while I'm not a strong believer in fate, I do know that sometimes timing is everything. And I also know—for certain—that time waits for no one.

Years ago, in the midst of me working twelve-hour days, seven days a week, my boss told me, "Greg, there are twenty-four hours in a day. You're only working from 7:00 a.m. to 7:00 p.m. That means there are still another twelve hours—half the day!—left. Hire another assistant."

He strongly believed that we could catch up on our sleep when we were dead (or at least he believed I could). I'm not actually promoting twenty-four-hour workdays, but sometimes we can fall victim to the passing of time, constantly dwelling on the lack thereof or all that we've lost. Consider this: though time has passed, there is still some left. What will you do with it?

Unfortunately, many of us are content with our current accomplishments or have resigned ourselves to believing we have experienced most of what life has to offer. If we have enjoyed good health, earned the support of our family and friends, and are able to provide for ourselves and family reasonably well, we consider this a good life. But is there more?

Do you have spare time? If you are honest with yourself, would you say you have time to waste? Are you wasting time? If we are going to live our fullest life, we have to have a curious attitude. If we're unwilling to reach out and explore, we're destined to live a familiar —although hopefully comfortable—life. And that's OK. There is good motivation and intention behind this, but if this is the path you choose, you have to live with the truth that you probably have it in you to do more, to become more, and to broaden your horizons.

While limited financial resources or time may mitigate our opportunities to proactively stretch our horizons or further develop diverse skills, this does not have to limit our internal growth or our willingness to take risks, pivot, or go all in. But to do this, we have to be receptive to these opportunities; sometimes, we have to get creative; and we definitely have to be open to saying yes.

When opportunities come your way, will you see them or know them?

I'm not done yet. As long as there is breath in my body, I have more to give, more to learn, more to love. People ask me if I'm ever going to retire and I say, "Retire from what?" I have always loved what I do for "work" and honestly view it more as a hobby than a job. I enjoy the idea of giving back, whether it's through time with my grandkids, helping people solve difficult business problems, or writing a book to help guide you on your journey—I think these are things that make life worth living.

There were times in my life when I was solely focused on a definitive destination—graduating from college, getting my CPA license, starting a business—but in the process of pursuing these end goals, I came to realize that there was much more to life than checking achievements off a list. Than feeding my insatiable ego. Than accumulating and rising and proving. I came to understand that there were so many gifts to unwrap on the path to attainment, values that began to define who I was and what I wanted to instill in those around me.

Particularly in the challenging moments—failing French, admitting defeat, making mistakes—I had to believe that there was meaning in the struggle. There was something for me to find, a key that would unlock other difficulties and other challenges down the road. Something that I could share with others to make their suffering just a little bit easier. Had I not believed this, I would have resigned to hopelessness. Believing this gave me the courage to persevere, to not quit, to grow and become. And to continue, even today.

Over time, the definitive destinations mattered less and less as I began to enjoy the process of getting there more than the achievement itself. And perhaps that's the most special key of them all—the realization that the journey itself is the destination. Keep on going. Don't give up. There's still time left.

A KEY: GRATITUDE

Question: Do you live a life of thankfulness?

Gratitude is like a skeleton key, a key that can open so many doors.

But gratitude is a *choice*. And the tricky thing about choice is that we can choose either way. You can choose to be grateful or you can choose to ignore gratitude altogether, to focus on the lack, to miss out on the good. As we practice gratitude, as we intentionally look for things to enjoy and savor, it becomes a state of mind. We become grateful people. That's when we start waking up each morning with a "carpe diem" mentality, with expectations for and engagement in all that the day will bring our way.

My parents taught me the true meaning of gratitude—not just being thankful when times are good or when there's obvious abundance, but having gratitude all the time, for everything that comes our way. It may seem odd to choose gratitude in the midst of suffering, but truly some of the worst moments of my life have led to the most meaningful relationships, the most profound understanding, and the most surprising opportunities that would not have been possible otherwise. Sometimes, we just don't know what a gift looks like.

As we start to see our hiccups and our failures in a new light, as part of the process of becoming, we begin to find gratitude in the very midst of struggle. Even when we haven't yet achieved what we set out to do. Even when we still don't understand the lesson that we're supposed to learn. Even when we still have a long way yet to go. When we can tap into thankfulness in these moments and *know* in our very depths that this is it—this is all part of the process of becoming—this is a marvelous place to be. Feel it! Believe it!

This is the key to getting older in a living way. This is the key that unlocks the journey becoming the destination.

CONCLUSION

ONE OF MY VERY FIRST TASKS for Levitt Palmer was to hire a full-time secretary for our headquarters (mind you, this was 1981, so they were still called secretaries back then); this person would report directly to me. I'll never forget the shock I felt when one of the interviewees said, "I have permanent PMS, so sometimes I'm not the easiest person to get along with, but you'll get over it."

I appreciated her forthcomingness. We hired her: Ms. Sally Thompson.

Twenty years later, when I went to work for the CPA firm to run their investment banking business, Sally came too. And then when I went to work for Ward Streeter, there was Sally. And after I moved to Las Vegas to work for Rick Hamilton, Sally eventually joined me down there too. Let's just say, she saw it all, and she was a great person to work with (and true to her word, I did get over her "permanent PMS").

I just got a note from her the other day. It said, "How are the kids? How are the grandkids? How's Kate? Next week is Boss's Day, and I just wanted to say that I really enjoyed working for you all those years. It was a lot of fun. But it wasn't easy."

It wasn't easy.

Ain't that the truth? I think we can be duped into thinking life is supposed to be smooth sailing all of the time. But where's the fun in that? We find out who we are when things get tough. We find out what's important to us and who will stick by us and what we're made of. And I think the real "fun" happens when we find ourselves in the middle of the hard stuff, when we have problems to solve, when we learn and grow, when we get to be a part of making the world just a little bit better.

WHAT'S NEXT?

One of Sally's favorite questions to ask me over the years was, "What are you going to do next?"

I remember it was eleven o'clock one night and we had just found out that we had three hundred people stranded in Cozumel, the plane was broken, and we didn't have a replacement. This had to be an awful experience for these people. They were done with vacation, at the airport ready to head home, with family awaiting their arrival and commitments to tend to the next day. They had entrusted us to get them home, but we had a very limited fleet and rarely had a spare plane without having to reroute a bunch of aircrafts.

"What are you going to do next?" she asked.

"Well, I've got the *Minneapolis Star* newspaper on the line."

"What are you going to do next?"

"We're going to tell the papers we need another plane. Hopefully we can charter someone else's plane to Cozumel to get them out."

And just like that, the founder of a competing charter airline called and said, "I heard you're stuck in Cozumel, but I can loan you a plane."

I said, "You are my hero. Can I tell the world that you're my hero?"

"Please do," he said.

Win. Win.

We all need a Sally sitting on our shoulder asking, "What are you going to do next?" It forces momentum, encourages problem-solving, puts you in the driver's seat. We have more control than we think. We just have to use our amazing brains to consider the options and our amazing hearts to consider how other people will be impacted. Regardless, every problem we face requires action, putting one foot in front of the other, and simply doing the next thing.

INVESTMENT

While many of the problems I faced during my career carried considerable financial weight, I hope you can see how to apply some of these keys to the way that you work through your own personal and professional problems, regardless of the tangible outcome. The values that drove my decision-making can be applied to any industry and any situation. Self-inspection, happiness, intuition, curiosity—these were keys to unlock a different way of thinking, not magic keys to access millions of dollars.

In truth, I believe you are your greatest investment—your mind, body, and spirit. Your relationships. What kind of commitment are you making to yourself? How are you applying all of these precious values to yourself? How are you investing into those around you?

If you know who you are and choose to be true to yourself, it will absolutely shape your life. It will impact your job, your family, your friendships, your community. It will change how you filter the plethora of information that bombards you every single day. It will help you make decisions with more clarity. You are worthy of attention, kindness, and care, and investing into yourself is ultimately an investment into a bright, happy future—for you and for everyone you impact.

CELEBRATE

I hope you have found something of value in these pages—a reminder that you have what it takes. I hope you are beginning to see your problems in a different light: as doors that you get to pass through to the next great adventure. I hope this adds an element of excitement to your life: both the assurance that you can unlock the door and, when you do, the realization that there is so much more on the other side. Your journey has begun again!

I'm well into my seventies, and I can tell you with confidence that the journey is, in fact, the destination. The everyday living—the getting up and working and playing and talking and listening and eating and enjoying—that's where the magic happens. We often get so focused on certain milestones—a promotion or a number in the bank account or a particular accomplishment—that we lose sight of the small things that make life so wonderful. These are moments to celebrate.

Solving a problem that you didn't think you could figure out, that's worth celebrating too. Finding out that you are more creative, innovative, and resilient than you thought, that's certainly worth celebrating. Making a great decision that honors other people, well, that's absolutely worth celebrating. Learning from a great big mess of a mistake that you caused—yes—even that's worth celebrating.

LIFE HAPPENS

You're likely going to set this book down and immediately get distracted by life—a crying kid or a baseball flying through your window or a Girl Scout knocking on your door to sell you more Thin Mints (do they even do that anymore?). Maybe you are taking a big, deep breath and thanking the gods that you will never find yourself in some of the situations Greg Smith had to piece together. That's good.

I hope you start reflecting on your choices differently. Not looking backward and dwelling on the past, second guessing decisions that are done, or getting caught up in the endless cycle of regret. There's no sense in beating yourself up over what has been. No, I want you to look forward, to consider the part you get to play in this great journey and who you are becoming. I want you to realize all that you can do and start solving problems from a posture of gratitude and empowerment.

And here we are, at the end of our journey together. And perhaps right smack-dab in front of another locked door. I have one more question for you here: what will you do next?

ACKNOWLEDGMENTS

WRITING A BOOK IS NO EASY TASK. Discovering a message that's worth writing about is even harder—it took me almost an entire lifetime! Thankfully, I didn't have to do it alone. If it weren't for the people along the way, I wouldn't have a thing to share. I am forever indebted to my family, friends, bosses, coworkers, employees, partners, neighbors, and even a few strangers. With that said, I want to acknowledge and celebrate the following people:

Mom and Dad, who lovingly taught me that my life was one worth living, despite the stupid things I did and said while growing up: Thank you for your endless and unconditional love, for setting boundaries, and enforcing consequences. For instilling in me self-esteem and self-respect and reminding me that, no matter what, better days would follow (and you were right). And for letting me make plenty of mistakes, not telling me answers but giving me just enough rope to figure things out myself.

A very special thanks to Kate, my amazing wife of fifty years (this year!), for indulging me with immeasurable support, patience, and love so that I could expand my life's journey without limits. You have never doubted me, even in the most difficult of times. And you are the most loved and respected mother to our two daughters and grandmother to our four grandchildren. How do you do it all?

Lindsay and Hillary, my forever two little girls, thank you for never once questioning my absences and for teaching me how to be a worthy father and friend. Cheers to you and your many successes, including marrying two guys who have become my best friends (thanks for picking good ones).

My four ACES—Ava, Cooper, Everett, and Sebastian—thank you for inspiring me every day to see a world of endless challenges and possibilities.

Gary and Patti, my younger brother and sister, who watched me flounder as the oldest of three and ratted me out only once, when I more than deserved it hundreds of times.

Kasim, who had the curiosity and courage to show up one day, not really knowing why. That one decision has led to a lifelong friendship, where the mentor has become the mentee. I am grateful to you and for you. Thanks also for the incredible gift of Scribe and the Scribe team assembled by Tucker Max, founder and president. I am glad you and Tucker met, as I am surely a beneficiary of that fateful encounter. Lastly, cheers Kasim to your continued success in everything you do and will do in the future. You do inspire. What a ride!

Zach, my business partner and friend whose business acumen and leadership gives our business practice legacy for the future.

Amir, my brother from another mother, thank you for showering me with encouragement.

Pete M. and Kelly M. and your amazing family, thank you for reinforcing what true friendship and family values mean to me.

The family patriarchs and business owners who I had the honor and pleasure of working with: thank you for trusting me with countless decisions along the way, standing by my side, and backing me up in the most challenging of times.

Joan J.—thank you for always putting our business schedules and commitments over your own and for grinding out work all hours of the day and night. You are forever in my hall of fame.

John Br., who worked in the trenches with me for nearly twenty years—thank you for your great wisdom along the way. You are a man of few words, and when you spoke, I listened.

Mark L., my dear friend who shares my family and business values—thank you for showing up in a full-length, snow-covered bearskin coat in the dead of winter to teach me what I didn't know about customer loyalty in the airline business and loyalty in friendship too.

To college friends who helped shape and broaden my opinions in the seventies: Lee L. (RIP), Greg M., Doug S., Kris S., Jim C., Elizabeth C., and many more.

To John S. (RIP), who allowed me to comanage with him what we believed was the most successful and FUN airline since Orville and Wilbur took off from Kitty Hawk. What an adventure we had over those nine years and thereafter.

George F. (RIP), you challenged almost every decision I made with "why" and taught me that it's better to do a few things really right than a bunch of things just average—what a priceless gift.

A big thank you to so many others that have shaped my story: Harold and Sheldon, my former business partners. Hadden (RIP), who always put others before himself and whose friendship I will always cherish. David and Geramin, Tim and Heidi, Kirsten and Ron, Roger and Vicki, John and Gretchen, and Doug and Nan, my international travel buddies who indulge my every curiosity. Zach S., Bob F., Rob F., Jim H., Lee S., Dean H., Dana J., David R., Mark P., Peter C., Steve A., Curt B., Tom S., Andrew P., Anthony H., Doug B., John R., John T., Joel G., Steve W., Jerry G., Ann H., John H., Mike M., Jean V., Josh G., Heidi S., and many more who have discovered they could unlock doors and become successful in every way.

To all the folks at Scribe: Emilie Jimenez, my friend and editor, who invested hundreds of hours in me to draw out the best parts of this book; Eliece Pool, my very patient publishing manager; Chelsea McGuckin, who captured my message in an image that became the cover of this book; and Barbara Boyd, executive editor extraordinaire.

And finally, Sister Nancy, who proffered up the subtitle for this book after a brief chance meeting in Oberammergau, Germany. Thank you for praying about it and sharing your insights. "Write this down," you said. And I did.

ABOUT THE AUTHOR

A true jack-of-all-trades, **GREGORY SMITH** is a financial advisor who has managed the business interests of ultra-high-net-worth families across several industries. He's led dozens of business mergers and acquisitions and been at the forefront of multiple bank acquisitions while leading challenging transactions in aviation, chemical, automobile, finance, real estate, and insurance. Greg has worked with regulatory agencies of all types, including the Treasury Department, the DOT, and the FAA.

Greg specializes in offering a nuanced perspective that considers all elements of a transaction, both human and financial. He draws on a vast array of experience to enable the best outcomes for all affected constituencies.

www.ingramcontent.com/pod-product-compliance
Lightning Source LLC
Chambersburg PA
CBHW060522080526
44586CB00012B/572